German–Texan Culinary Art
When Everything Was *Hausgemacht*

REZEPTE

by
NEVILEE MAASS WEAVER

EAKIN PRESS · Austin, Texas

FIRST EDITION

Copyright © 1999
By Nevilee Maass Weaver

Published in the United States of America
By Eakin Press
An Imprint of Sunbelt Media, Inc.
P.O. Drawer 90159 ★ Austin, TX 78709-0159
email: eakinpub@sig.net
website: www.eakinpress.com

ISBN 1-57168-248-1

Library of Congress Cataloging-in-Publication Data

Rezepte : passing them on to the next generation / compiled by Nevilee Maass
Weaver ; translations by Nevilee Maass Weaver.
    p.   cm.
Includes index.
ISBN 1-57168-248-1 (hard)
    1. Cookery, German. I. Weaver, Nevilee Maass, 1928-.
TX721.R33   1999
641.5943--dc21   98-48361
                                                          CIP

DEDICATION

This book is dedicated to
my Texas German family and friends and
especially to my Mother, Caroline Brauner Maass;
my Father, Fritz (Friedrich) Maass;
my grandmothers, Anna Mertin Brauner and
Julia Schoenfeld Maass;
my maternal aunts,
Anna Brauner Alaminsky,
Elizabeth Brauner Alaminsky, Frieda Brauner Kraemer,
Hilda Brauner Schultz, Hedwig Brauner Vogler,
Agnes Brauner Williams;
and my maternal uncle, Alfred Brauner.

GEBRATENEN
TAUBEN FLIEGEN
EINEM NICHT
INS MAUL.

It won't be
handed to you
on a platter.

Contents

693651

DATE	8-16-03

NAME Mafine Vara

ADDRESS		ORDER NO.	

CITY, STATE, ZIP

SOLD BY	CASH	C.O.D.	CHARGE	ON ACCT.	MDSE. RETD.	PAID OUT

QUAN.	DESCRIPTION	PRICE	AMOUNT
1	1 Rezepte	15 95	15 95
2			
3			
4			
5			
6			
7			
8			
9			
10			
11			
12			
13			
14			

RECEIVED BY

	TAX	1 32
	TOTAL	17 27

adams 24705

PREFACE

In 1976 a collection of my Tante Lisa (Elizabeth) Alaminsky's recipes written in the old German script was given to me. In the process of putting her estate in order, her children—Lawrence Alaminsky, Selma Draemer, and Evelyn Vaclavik—found the recipes in a drawer in her kitchen. Since none of them could read German, they weren't sure just what they should do with them. Evelyn suggested that these treasured recipes be given to me, because I could read German; Lawrence and Selma agreed. I was deeply touched by their gift, and I felt a real responsibility to share them with others.

I read them carefully. I reviewed in my mind some recipes my Mother passed on to me orally. I re-read recipes from other Texas-German homemakers of that era in my files. These recipes are fundamental; they have not been adapted to new ways and modern ingredients. In them, I discovered a rich source of our heritage that should not be lost. Therefore, after more than twenty years of contemplation, I set to work to compile a book made up of a number of these recipes. They are presented in their original forms, as nearly as possible, in English.

I am so grateful for Lawrence, Slema, and Evelyn's gift to me, and to the many others who have shared their recipes with me through the years. While working on this project, I valued the help, encouragement, and support of my daughter-in-law, Mary Weaver, and my sons, Donald and Perry Weaver. My warmest gratitude goes to each one of them. One of the delights of working on this book was the interest of my grand-children, Ray and Travy Weaver. They were an inspiration, and I thank them for that.

Now that this collection of heritage recipes is available to be explored and enjoyed, I ask that it be passed on to the next generation. A fragment of our Texan-German heritage will then be preserved.

NEVILEE MAASS WEAVER

EARLY
TEXAN-GERMAN COOKERY

DAS SCHMECKT NACH MEHR.
(That tempts one to eat more.)

Germans immigrated to Texas for a number of reasons: political oppression, religious persecution, bad economic conditions, and the desire to escape military service. The Germans began settling in Texas while it was a Mexican province. Some of them dreamed of establishing a "New Germany" in Texas; that dream died. These early settlers largely clung to their native language and culture. Yet they liked their adopted land and readily proclaimed allegiance to the United States of America. These immigrants insisted that their children learn the English language. This polarization, that is, their love of the German language and culture and their love for their adopted country, coupled with the desire to become Americanized, is reflected in their food.

Many of the early German settlers became successful farmers. Their gardens produced a variety of vegetables. They grew the familiar cabbages, turnips, potatoes, and green beans. The relatively unfamiliar eggplant and okra were grown from seeds given them by American neighbors.

The homemakers' responsibility was to prepare meals using home-grown produce. The foods prepared retained the distinctive characteristics of the "old country." Like their ancestors, they relied upon the natural good taste of the food rather than complicated cooking methods. The cooks considered a little salt and pepper or a dash of nutmeg enough seasoning for most gravies.

They exchanged recipes with their American neighbors. From them, they learned how to cook okra and eggplant, as well as American ways to prepare other foods. For example, rice cooked according to a neighbor's recipe was *Reis auf amerikanische Art* (rice American style). The combination of traditional German and American foods made Texan-German cookery pleasantly familiar to Americans.

Homemakers took great pride in their cakes and pastries. Generally they didn't have the molds for *Springerle* or fancy cakes. Nor did they have the time or skills to form intricate little flowers, fruits, or animals out of marzipan dough. They quickly adapted to the limitations of their kitchens, equipment, and the available ingredients. They created molasses-sweetened dough, which was rolled out and cut into fat round cookies with a glass whenever no other cookie cutter was available. Raisins, nuts, and beaten egg whites decorated them. Rich buttery layer cakes were born, along with heavy, rich fruit cakes which could be stored for months without refrigeration. A friendly rivalry sprung up between homemakers. They put hearts and souls into their homemade cakes trying to "out do" each other.

Bread was the Germans' basic food in the "old country;" it remained so in Texas. Bread to them meant a white bread made with wheat flour and yeast. All other breads were defined by the grain from which they were baked. Baking bread involved mixing, kneading, letting the dough rise, punching it down, shaping it into loaves, letting them rise, and then baking the loaves. In cold weather this process often took two days because of the slowness of the dough to rise. The homemaker usually set aside one day a week to bake bread. Even today the aroma of baking bread causes their descendants to become nostalgic.

The farm provided a variety of meat for the table. The

ALLER ANFANG IST SCHWER.
(Every beginning is difficult.)

settlers fattened hogs to be slaughtered during the cold months of the year both to prevent spoiling and to allow time for processing. An inherent frugality made sure they used every ounce of the hog, from the snout to the tail, in some way. It was cooked fresh, made into sausages, hams, bacon, preserved in lard, smoked, or pickled.

The main course of the meal, particularly on festive occasions and Sundays, was often chicken, turkey, duck, or goose. During the immigrant's first years in America, a roast goose stuffed with an apple and raisin dressing took center place on Christmas day. They also brought a fondness for duck with them. These birds were roasted with stuffings of apples and sometimes prunes. As the years went by, a roasted turkey became the main course of holiday meals. Roasted, fried, or stewed chicken was a Sunday dinner staple.

In some sections of Texas, the "Beef Club" served as an important source of fresh meat during the summer. A "Beef Club" was a group of farmers who took turns slaughtering a steer each Saturday. The dressed beef was taken to the farm of the member who served as the butcher. They rotated the cut of beef a member received each week, so that every family could enjoy the better cuts of meat during the course of the season.

The family fisherman and hunter supplied wild game. Fish rolled in cornmeal and fried in hot fat until crisp was relished. The noon meal might feature rabbits and squirrels baked, fried, or made into a hearty stew. A haunch of venison roasted to perfection and spicy venison sausages fed family and friends quite well.

While much is heard about the German's preference for beer, the rumored "basic food," it did not play a starring role on the homemaker's menu. Some families brewed beer at home. Farmers also produced excellent wine from whatever grapes (often wild mustang grapes), fruits, or berries, were available. They aged and stored the wines in hand crafted wine cellars. A good cup of coffee, however, was the beverage of choice. A steaming cup, accompanied by delectable home-baked cake or pastry, was a pleasant treat not to be passed up.

Ordinarily the traditional "old country" breakfast of rolls,

> *ISS WAS GAR IST, TRINK WAS KLAR IST,*
> *SPRICH WAS WAHR IST.*
> (Eat what's cooked, drink what's clear,
> speak the truth.)

butter, jam, eggs cooked in their shells, cheese, or sausage, was not served in Texas. The bacon and egg breakfast of their American neighbors became the morning fare.

At noon, the big meal of the day, the table was heaped with meat, potatoes, vegetables, fruit, bread, and pudding. The evening meal consisted of leftovers from the noon meal or a simple meal of fried potatoes, milk, bread, and cold meat.

During the weekend, and especially on Sundays, a fourth meal, *lunch* was added. *Lunch* fell between midday and evening, with guests frequently being invited. They served coffee with tasty home-baked cakes and pastries. They added to this fare trays of sandwiches made of meat salad, slices of meat, or cheese. Cakes and pastries were rarely offered as dessert at the end of dinner, but rather were saved for this occasion. Sometimes just cake and coffee made up the menu.

Thus the cooking of our Texan-German ancestors was solid and basic, but really good and satisfying. The early settlers set a bountiful table. Guests would say *"Wir befinden uns hier recht gemuetlich"* ("We feel very comfortable here"). Good nature, geniality, pleasantness, kindliness, comfort, and coziness pervaded—that's *Gemuetlichkeit.*

HANDING DOWN THE RECIPES

This book consists of a collection of recipes used by German settlers from the late 1800s to the early 1900s. It's not an exhaustive collection. Some readers may miss their favorites, or question the ingredients used to prepare a dish. That favorite recipe can, however, be written on the pages provided for that purpose. As a general rule, no recipe has a special name. It was referred to simply as layer cake, fruit cake, chicken salad, green peas, or some other general title.

The language and measures used in the recipes indicate that they were written by immigrants after they came to America. In a number of instances, they used English words in place of German. For example, the writer used the English word, 'salmon,' instead of the German words, *Salm* or *Lachs.* The immigrants liked to use English words in this way because they felt it added a touch of sophistication. Sometimes they couldn't think of a German word for the English word, or no such food existed in Germany. In that case, they either used the English word, or they made up something that sounded German. For example, "Gumbo" became "Gombo." When the immigrants wrote down their recipes in German, they generally used the American system of measurements, instead of the metric measures commonly used in Germany. While translating, an effort was made to retain the style and feeling indicated by the language of the unknown writer of each recipe.

Usually the cooks added to, or subtracted from, a basic recipe. That is, they created their own version of the recipe. In some instances, variations for a number of the same dishes are presented. The measures used in these recipes are frequently not standard; a cup may mean a large coffee cup or a small tea cup, a spoon may be a soup spoon or a dessert spoon. Vague terms in the recipes such as "strong fire, good heat, moderate oven" tell what cooking temperature should be used. When using these recipes, adjustments must be made. Consequently, different people using the same recipe will rarely get identical results. So think of these recipes as guidelines and follow your own taste and preference.

Trying these recipes will be an adventure. Through them one will discover the joys of the good basic cooking of our Texan-German ancestors. One learns that our forefathers ate quite well. Most important, the natural good taste of the food will prove a very pleasant experience. Pass it on to the next generation! GUTEN APPETIT!

THE GERMAN PROVERBS

Every language has its proverbs, colloquial expressions, and idioms. Like other cultures, the Germans use them to make a point, teach children, or just have fun. They also use them to convey wisdom and preserve their beliefs, traditions, and customs.

Some German proverbs are not that different from English ones. The words may not, at times, lend themselves to a literal translation, but the essential meaning and intention defies cultural barriers and thereby shows what values the two ethnicities hold in common. Here are some examples.

Aus dem Augen, aus dem Sinn.
(Out of sight, out of mind.)

Wer nicht arbeitet, soll nicht essen.
(He who does not work, neither shall he eat.)

Wo ein Wille ist, ist auch ein Weg.
(Where there's a will, there's a way.)

Regional colloquialisms and idioms when used in everyday language add a distinctive flavor, charm, and humor to conversations. When something has gone wrong, or is unbelievable, a German might say: *Ach du liebe Zeit* (Good gracious)! or *Ach du lieber Himmel* (Good heavens)! *Fluessiges Brot* (liquid bread) is one way to describe beer. *Schafskopf* (sheep's head) means one who is dull or stupid; a dumbbell.

Choosing the appropriate proverbs for this book was no easy task; there are so many of them. I was "making a mountain out of a molehill." Or as the Germans say it *"Aus der Muecke einen Elfanten machen."* The final choices not only reveal the character of the people, but often relate to the subject matter. The German version of the proverb or expression is listed along with an equivalent English proverb or expression. The English phrase will usually not be a word for word translation, but rather what one would use in everyday speech.

But literal translations add humor and insight. For example, *"Aus der Muecke einen Elfanten machen."* is "To make an elephant out of a gnat." Thus a literal translation may be found above some of the English equivalents in parentheses.

DER BACKOFEN
(THE OVEN)

A cast-iron cooking range fueled by wood held a prominent place in the homes of German settlers in Texas. The range consisted of a top with round, movable plates and an oven for baking. The family used it to prepare food and as a source of warmth during the winter. A tin stovepipe carried the smoke from the burning fire out through the roof. The stove had to be stoked regularly to maintain the oven's heat.

Keeping the range heated for cooking was a challange. Maintaining it, however, was an ongoing chore. Fine, black soot clung to the inside of the stovepipe. Mounds of ashes accumulated in the wood burning chamber. The range needed frequent attention to function well. Since the Germans believed cleanliness was next to godliness, the range had to be scrubbed, then rubbed with a pasty, smelly black polish until it gleamed.

The ovens had no thermostats. Cooks used terms such as slow, moderate, and hot oven to describe baking tempetures. Today's recipes, however, give precise oven temperatures. The following guidelines should be helpful:

Slow oven (240 to 325 degrees)
Moderate oven (325 to 400 degrees)
Quick-or hot-oven (400 to 450 degrees)
Very hot oven (450 to 550 degrees)

Those who have an oven with a questionable thermostat will find the old fashioned method of determining oven temperatures to be useful. Sprinkle flour on a flat pan and put into a heated oven. In a *slow* oven, the flour turns light brown in five minutes. In a *moderate* oven, the flour turns medium brown in five minutes. In a *hot* oven, the flour turns dark brown in five minutes. In a *very hot* oven, the flour turns dark brown in three minutes.

GEBETE
(PRAYERS)

VOR DEM ESSEN
(BEFORE MEALS)

Komm Herr Jesu sei unser Gast
Und segnet was du uns bescheret hast.
Amen

Come Lord Jesus be our guest
And let Thy gifts to us be blest.
Amen

NACH DEM ESSEN
(AFTER MEALS)

Wir danken Dir Herr Gott mit
demuetigen Herzen fuer alle Deine
Guete und Barmherzigkeit.
Amen

We thank Thee Lord God, with humble
hearts for thy goodness and mercy.
Amen

GOTT HILFT DENEN, DIE SICH SELBST HELFEN.
(God helps those who help themselves.)

FLEISCH

MEAT

"Koch Tips" From Long Ago

When baking stuffed chickens in the oven, they will stay stuffed, if the cavity is closed up with clean wire hairpins.

If one has trouble removing pinfeathers from poultry, try using a pair of eyebrow tweezers.

A teaspoonful of lemon juice added to the water before boiling chicken helps to make it tender.

A pinch of baking soda added to the water in which chicken is soaking improves its flavor.

To make most meats tender when cooked, rub them with vinegar when raw.

To make a tough steak tender, rub it on both sides with a mixture of vinegar and olive oil, and let it stand two hours before cooking.

To make a ham tender, leave it in the water in which it has been boiled, until cold. This will also make it juicier.

The flavor of boiled ham can be improved by wrapping it in buttered paper and baking it for an hour.

To make meats and vegetables more tender, and to cook them quickly, put a pinch of cooking soda in the water when boiling them.

Boil sausages about eight minutes before frying them, or roll them in flour before frying them, to prevent them from breaking or shrinking.

Every bit of fat from scraps of meat, bacon drippings, roasts, soups, and poultry may be made into a mixture for general cooking purposes.

To keep hot fat from spattering, sprinkle a little flour or salt in it before frying.

To draw the juice out of meat, add cold water. To hold the juice in, add hot water.

When pounding tough meat, pound flour into it to prevent the valuable juices from escaping.

To prevent fish from sticking to the bottom of the pan when frying, sprinkle a little salt over the bottom of the pan.

> ## *ER IST EIN BLINDES HUHN.*
> ## HE IS AS BLIND AS A CHICKEN.
> ### (He is blind as a bat.)

A GERMAN proverb says "the most important vegetable in the world is meat." This typifies the hard working German Texans' attitude toward meat. Furthermore, they weren't all that fond of complicated meat dishes. They clung to what they were used to, and were sometimes accused of not wanting to change. Platters of steaming, slowly boiled or slowly roasted game, beef, pork or poultry were ordinarily served for the noon meal. For breakfast they usually ate cured ham, thick slices of fried bacon, or heated sausages. Leftover meat was warmed up for supper.

GEFUELLETES HUHN
(STUFFED CHICKEN)

Dress the chicken carefully and wash it, but do not cut it open too much. Filling: Chop onion, liver, heart, and gizzard very fine, then add a handful of seedless raisins, some softened white bread, 1 egg yolk, some butter, a little salt and pepper; mix together well. Stuff filling into chicken; sew closed. Put chicken in a pan containing a mixture of ½ melted butter and ½ melted lard to bake. One must turn the chicken often and baste with the sauce. To this sauce, one may add some corn starch and spices.

BACKOFEN-GEBRATENES HUHN
(OVEN-FRIED CHICKEN)

Melt some lard and butter in a pan. Mix some flour, salt and pepper; coat pieces of frying chicken with it. Arrange chicken skin side down in shorting and butter. Bake uncovered in a hot oven. Turn chicken once while baking.

GEKOCHTE ZUNGE
(COOKED TONGUE)

Clean the tongue thoroughly, then cook in salted water until done. Cut into thin slices. The sauce for it is made from water, seedless raisins, lard, pepper, an onion, some spices, and corn starch.

ZUBEREITUNG DES GEHIRNS
(PREPARATION OF BRAINS)

Take 1 pound brains, 6 eggs, pepper, and onions. Chop the brains, then fry them in butter with onions until done. Beat eggs well and add to the brains while on the fire. Stir until done.

HUNGARISCHER GULASCH
(HUNGARIAN GOULASH)

Rub pan with butter. Place thinly sliced potatoes, onions, cooked meat cut into bite size pieces, salt, and pepper in alternate single layers in pan. Then pour a can of tomatoes over it. Bake 1 hour.

FARMER-STEW
(FARMER'S STEW)

This dish requires a thick slice of beef from the hindquarter. Sprinkle meat with flour. Pound it into the meat, so that the flour penetrates the meat and absorbs the juice. During the pounding, always sprinkle more flour onto the meat until it absorbs no more. In the meantime, put lard and tallow in a meat kettle, and let it get very hot. Put the meat into this hot fat over a strong fire and brown it on both sides. Then add enough boiling water to just barely cover the meat. Put a tight fitting lid on the kettle. Stew the meat for 2 to 2 ½ hours over low heat. Season to taste with salt and pepper. A cup of tomato sauce may be added immediately or just before serving.

RINDERBRATEN
(BEEF POT ROAST)

Season a 4-pound chuck or rump roast with salt and pepper; add onions and brown meat on all sides in hot fat. Put browned meat on a platter. Brown the flour in the fat. When flour is brown, add water and a bay leaf and cook. Put the browned meat into the gravy, which should cover the meat. Put a lid on the pot, and cook it in a moderate oven for 2 to 3 hours or until tender.

GEBRATENE LEBER
(FRIED LIVER)

Pull the skin off the liver and cut liver into very thin slices. Sprinkle with salt and pepper and roll in flour. Fry in medium hot fat. Make a sauce out of fat, browned flour, 2 sliced onions, salt and pepper.

LEBERWURST ZU BUTTERBROT
(LIVER SAUSAGE FOR BREAD AND BUTTER)

Grind 1 raw pork liver fine, or lay the liver in boiling

ES GEHT UM DIE WURST.

THERE IS A SAUSAGE AT STAKE.

(It's a question of now or never.)

broth for a few minutes, and rub it through a sieve. Chop 2 parts of boiled pork and fat to 1 part of liver. Mix the pork and liver; season to taste with salt, black pepper, allspice, and nutmeg. Fill the mixture into thick flat pork casings. Leave a 2 finger wide space in the casings. Hang sausages on a rod; suspend rod over boiling water with the sausages immersed in boiling water. Slowly cook for a ½ hour. While cooking gently push sausages into the water with a flat spoon to keep them from bursting. Sausages may be served smoked or not smoked. To smoke the sausages, hang a good distance from the fire in a strong smoke for eight to ten days. After smoking, hang them in an airy frost free place to store.

BOCKWURST
(VENISON SAUSAGE)

Use equal parts of ground venison and ground pork. Sprinkle salt, pepper, and saltpeter over the meat and mix well. Red pepper and garlic may be added as desired. Stuff into pork casings. To smoke the sausages, hang a good distance from fire in a strong smoke.

BLUTWURST
(BLOOD SAUSAGE)

Beat warm blood fresh from the hog with a whisk until it is cool. Stir blood through a sieve so that it remains fluid. Add cooked, finely chopped lean and fat pork, finely chopped pork skins, and bacon which is cut into small cubes to a part of the blood. Season with salt, black pepper, cloves, and allspice. Mix well. Put mixture in the thickest possible smooth pork casings. Don't stuff too tightly because the mixture expands as it cooks. Boil in water for a ½ hour. Smoke some to serve with butter and bread. Since some men don't like the cubes of bacon, chop the bacon finely. If bacon isn't put in the sausage, it will be dry.

FRISCHE BRATWURST
(FRESH FRIED SAUSAGE)

Pour boiling water over sausages and let stand about 15 minutes; remove from water; place sausage in a pan; prick with a fork. Put in oven and cook until brown, or cook in a frying pan until brown.

IM PFEFFER SEIN.

TO BE IN A PEPPER.

(To be in a pickle or a jam.)

GEPICKELTE SCHWEINEFUESSE
(PICKLED PIG'S FEET)

Clean 4 good-sized pig's feet; cover with hot water. Simmer until meat falls from bones. Take feet out of the water. Remove the largest bones from the boiled feet; put feet into a stone crock. Save water in which the feet boiled until later. Heat 1 quart strong vinegar with 4 bay leaves, 1 tablespoon whole cloves, 1 tablespoon broken cinnamon sticks, some salt and pepper, a blade of mace, and an onion cut in quarters. Simmer this mixture for about 45 minutes. Cool. Remove cake of fat from the top of the water in which feet had cooked. Add about 1 quart of this water to vinegar. Strain liquid through a sieve and pour over the feet in the stone crock. Chill for at least 2 days.

FLEISCH AUFZUBEWAHREN
(TO PRESERVE MEAT)

Bring good lard to a boil, then take 1 inch to 2 inches thick pieces of meat sprinkled with salt and pepper; lay it in the hot fat and let it fry well on both sides. Don't lay too much meat into the fat at one time. Otherwise, the fat will cool too much and too much juice will be drawn from the meat. The hot fat must close the pores of the meat immediately when it is laid into the fat. One never adds water. Lay the fried pieces of meat in a tin or crockery container. Cover with clean hot lard. Do not cover the container. Store in a cool place. Meat prepared in this way keeps well. Pork fried in June still tastes like fresh meat in late autumn.

GEFUELLTE PFEFFERSCHOTEN
(STUFFED PEPPERS)

Mix finely chopped cooked meat and 1 cup of bread softened in water. Add 2 well beaten eggs, salt, and black pepper to taste. This makes enough for 12 medium sized pods. Wash pods well; cut the stem ends from the pods; remove all seeds; fill each pod with the meat mixture. Put the stuffed peppers in a pan with some fat; let them bake in an oven until done.

GEFUELLTE KARTOFFELN
(STUFFED POTATOES)

Cut the top off big peeled potatoes. Core with an apple corer. Then make a stuffing of leftover pork roast chopped as fine as possible; mix with 1 egg, 1 tablespoon of sour cream, some onions, salt and ground mace to taste. Stuff the potatoes. Put the top on the potatoes and fasten with a string. Bake the stuffed potatoes in melted butter until done.

—or—

Sauté finely chopped meat and parsley in butter. Cool, then mix with some sour cream, salt, pepper and 2 eggs. Cut a thin piece (a top) off of the flat side of average sized baking potatoes. Hollow potatoes with a spoon. Fill the potatoes with the meat mixture and put the tops back on the potatoes. Steam slowly in a frying pan.

GEFUELLTER KOHLKOPF
(STUFFED CABBAGE)

Remove quite a few large leaves from a large head of white cabbage. Cook the leaves about 10 minutes. Lay a clean cloth in a colander. Then line the colander quite thickly with the cooked cabbage leaves from which the large stems have been removed.

Stuffing: The stuffing is prepared from lean beef which has been finely chopped, pepper, salt, some mace, a piece of butter melted and browned, some white bread which has been softened in cold water and has been squeezed out, and 2 eggs. Mix everything together well.

Layer meat mixture alternately with cabbage leaves in the colander until a big cabbage head is formed. Tie the four corners of the cloth together with a string. Immerse the wrapped cabbage head completely in lightly salted water and simmer over low heat for 2 hours until done. To serve, remove cabbage carefully from the cloth; put it on a dish. Pour sauce over it.

Sauce: Mix flour and melted butter, add meat broth, and juice of one lemon. Add a little of the hot mixture into a beaten egg yolk. Make sure it is cool enough that it doesn't cook the egg. Stir in flour mixture to make the sauce.

DAS MACHT DEN KOHL NICHT FETT.

THAT WON'T MAKE THE CABBAGE FAT.

(That doesn't help much.)

❁

AUFGEWAERMTER KOHL.

WARMED UP CABBAGE.

(Same old story.)

SCREIBEN SIE IHR LIEBLINGSREZEPT HIER!
WRITE YOUR FAVORITE RECIPE HERE!

PASS IT ON TO THE NEXT GENERATION!

SOSSE

SAUCE

"Koch Tips" From Long Ago

Take the lumps out of brown sugar by steaming it in a double boiler.

A good way to get stiff, firm whipped cream is to put three or four drops of lemon juice per cup into the cream before beating.

To brown flour, spread a thin layer on a dry shallow pan over low heat, stirring occasionally until browned.

To make brown gravies use browned flour.

More browned flour must be used than white flour to thicken a sauce.

If a sauce is too thick, it can be thinned by adding more water, and stirring constantly.

If sauce is lumpy, strain it.

Crush fresh green spinach leaves, tie them in a cloth, and squeeze out the juice. Add the juice to a soup or sauce a few minutes before serving for a green color.

Strained tomato juice will give soups and sauces a red color.

To keep thickened sauces hot, place over hot water until ready to use.

Reheating gravy or cooking it some more usually makes it thick and pasty.

To keep an opened bottle of olive oil from getting rancid, put a lump of sugar in each pint.

To substitute cream for butter: 1 cup light cream equals 2/3 cup skim milk plus 1/3 cup butter; 1 cup heavy cream equals 1/2 cup skim milk plus 1/2 cup butter.

The old trick of greasing the mouth of the cream pitcher with butter really will keep liquid from dripping.

Carrots can be peeled easily with a coarse grater.

To save time when peeling potatoes to be boiled, peel only

a strip around the potato lengthwise. The skin will come off easily when the potato is cooked.

GERMAN COOKS have always valued the good natural flavor of foods; sauces were used only when deemed necessary to enhance natural flavors. Since the Texan-German homemakers often did not have the time nor the ingredients available to make special sauces, they weren't all that popular. The sour taste of vinegar and the pungent flavor of mustard were favored in their sauces. All too often the sauce simply consisted of water, fat, and flour seasoned with salt.

SOSSE ZUM BLUMENKOHL (SAUCE FOR CAULIFLOWER)

Take 2 egg yolks, 1 tablespoon flour, 1 cup sweet cream, ½ cup of milk, 1 little piece of butter, some nutmeg, and 2 tablespoons of broth from the cauliflower. Mix together and beat until creamy. Pour the sauce over the cauliflower. Turnips can also be prepared this way.

TOMATO-CATSUP (TOMATO KETCHUP)

Take 1 bushel of tomatoes, cut them up, and cook them until they are soft. Rub them through a sieve, add ½ gallon of the best vinegar, 1 pint salt, ¼ pound cloves, ¼ pound allspice, 1 tablespoon of black pepper, 1 tablespoon of red pepper, and 5 cloves of garlic. Boil until quantity is reduced to a half. Beat

> GEFEFFERTER PREIS.
> PEPPERED PRICE.
> (Exorbitant price.)

well. Pour into little bottles. Seal with a cork. In this way, one can preserve tomato ketchup for a year.

REIFE GURKEN-CATSUP
(RIPE CUCUMBER KETCHUP)

Peel and grate 3 dozen ripe cucumbers. Drain the juice which accumulates while grating. Grate 2 onions for each quart of grated cucumbers. Combine grated cucumbers and onions. Add 1 teaspoon red pepper, 1 teaspoon black pepper, 1 teaspoon salt, 1/2 teaspoon ground cloves and 1 pint vinegar which has been boiled and cooled. Stir everything thoroughly. Fill little air tight bottles with mixture.

CHILI-SOSSE
(CHILI SAUCE)

Take 20 large ripe tomatoes, 6 large onions, 3 large green peppers, 3 spoonfuls of salt, 6 spoonfuls of brown sugar, 3 spoonfuls of ground cinnamon, 2 teaspoonfuls of ground ginger, 1/2 teaspoon of ground cloves, and 6 cups of vinegar. Mash the tomatoes and chop the onions; put them into a kettle. Cook ingredients until vegetables are soft. Beat thoroughly, and cook it like ketchup. Fill little bottles with the sauce. Cork the bottles well. Store them in the cellar or another dark place. Serve with roasts and poultry.

SOSSE FUER FISCH
(SAUCE FOR FISH)

Blend some butter and flour over a low fire. Don't brown. Add white wine or meat broth until a smooth sauce is formed.

EIN FROHES HERZ, GESUNDES BLUT,
IST BESSER ALS VIEL GELD UND GUT.
(A happy heart and healthy blood
is better than money and wealth.)

Add salt, nutmeg, and white pepper to taste. Finally, add the juice of 1 lemon and 2 or 3 beaten egg yolks. Stir until smooth.

MAYONAISE OHNE OEL
(MAYONNAISE WITHOUT OIL)

Mix well ½ cup sugar, some salt, ½ teaspoon dried mustard, some pepper, and 1 teaspoon flour. Melt 2 tablespoons lard over a low fire. (Don't let melted lard get hot.) Blend ingredients listed above into the melted lard. Slowly add ½ cup hot vinegar. Boil until mixture thickens. Remove from the fire. Slowly add 2 or 3 beaten egg yolks to the hot mixture. Use this mayonnaise over chopped cabbage or any other salad.

MAYONAISE
(MAYONNAISE)

Blend 1 cup vinegar, 1 tablespoon butter, 1 teaspoon powdered mustard, 1 teaspoon salt, 1 teaspoon pepper, 1 tablespoon sugar, and 1 egg. Mix well and bring to a boil.

ESSIGSOSSE ZU KOCHFLEISCH
(VINEGAR SAUCE FOR COOKED MEAT)

Blend some browned flour with water or bouillon until smooth. Season to taste with some salt, sugar, vinegar, and finely chopped parsley.

PETERSILIEN SOSSE FUER GEMUESE
(PARSLEY SAUCE FOR VEGETABLES)

Wash and scald parsley, squeeze out, and chop fine. Blend some melted butter and flour; add meat broth, 2 egg yolks, some parsley, some spoons of cream. Cook to thicken. Pour over vegetables.

> ## OHNE SAAT KEINE ERNTE.
> ## WITHOUT SOWING NO HARVEST.
> ### (As ye have sown, so shall ye reap.)

SCREIBEN SIE IHR
LIEBLINGSREZEPT HIER!
WRITE YOUR FAVORITE RECIPE HERE!

_____

_____

_____

_____

_____

_____

_____

_____

_____

_____

_____

_____

_____

_____

_____

_____

_____

_____

_____

_____

_____

_____

_____

_____

_____

_____

_____

_____

PASS IT ON TO THE NEXT GENERATION!

SUPPE UND SALAT

SOUP AND SALAD

"KOCH TIPS" FROM LONG AGO

To make good soup stock, slowly simmer together a mixture of 1/3 bones and 2/3 meat in water with seasoning for a long time to extract all the flavor.

Pour hot soup through a cloth rinsed in cold water to remove fat from the soup.

Add a turnip to correct a soup with too much onion flavor; cook the soup a bit more.

Onions will not make the eyes water if scalding water is poured over them before they are peeled.

Let cabbage, lettuce, cauliflower, or greens stand in cold salt water for an hour before using to draw out hidden insects.

Add a little vinegar or a pinch of borax to the water in which vegetables are being washed. Any live insects will come to the surface at once.

To test the age of an egg, place it in a deep pot of cold water. If it lies on its side it is fresh; if it stands at an angle, it is three or four days old; if it stands on end it is at least 10 days old. Any egg that floats on the surface is seldom fit to use.

For onion seasoning, plant a few sprouting onions in a pot. The shoots which appear can be snipped off for seasoning. Other shoots will soon grow in their place.

A quick way to get rid of onion or garlic oder on a knife is to run it through a potato.

Oranges are much easier to peel if placed in the oven for a moment before serving them.

Peaches, tomatoes, and beets can be easily skinned if boiling water is poured over them. Let them stand in it for a few minutes.

Lemon juice poured over pared fruit will prevent it from turning brown.

To make lemons give more juice, cook them in hot water for a few minures before squeezing.

To throughly season a wooden salad bowl for salad making, don't wash the bowl, but wipe it dry with a cloth.

THE GERMAN settlers were frugal. When making soup, they used what they had on hand. They added a little of this and a little of that to the soup pot. Soup ingredients weren't measured. For a thick soup, they added flour. For a thin soup, they added milk or water. They seasoned soups according to taste. Therefore, use the following soup recipes as a guide. Make your own choices, and use your own taste just as these early cooks did.

NUDELN
(NOODLES)

Put about 2 cups flour and some salt in a big bowl. Beat 1 or 2 eggs slightly with a little water. Make a well in the flour and salt mixture. Pour the water and egg mixture into the well. Use hands to make a very stiff smooth dough; divide it into 3 or 4 equal parts, and roll out each part into very thin sheets. Lay on a clean cloth to let it dry out some; roll the 3 or 4 pieces of dough up like a jelly roll. Slice the roll into thin noodles with a sharp knife; let dry. Boil in salted water or soup until done.

HUEHNERBRUEHE
(CHICKEN BROTH)

Cut an old hen into pieces (an old hen is more flavorful). Put the pieces in a kettle with cold water; add salt and pepper.

Vegetables such as carrots, celery, or onions may also be added. Cook until meat falls from the bones. Strain. Serve the broth hot. The meat may be used for chicken salad.

HUEHNERBRUEHE MIT REIS
(CHICKEN BROTH WITH RICE)

Heat chicken broth in a pot. Add some rice and cook until rice is fluffy. Serve hot.

> *DIE SUPPE AUSESSEN MUESSEN.*
>
> THE SOUP MUST ALL BE EATEN.
>
> (You have to abide by the consequences.)

HUEHNERSUPPE
(CHICKEN SOUP)

Cut a 3 to 4 pound old chicken into pieces. Cover chicken pieces with salted water. Cook until almost done. Add a few peppercorns, a bay leaf, and some parsley; cook until meat is well done. Cook about 3 cups of noodles in boiling salted water until tender. When done, drain noodles, put them into the pot with chicken. Serve chicken pieces on a platter, or leave them in the soup.

FLEISCHBRUEHE
(BEEF BROTH)

Place a pound or more shin of beef with bone into a large pot with chopped onions, chopped carrots, chopped celery, a little chopped parsley, salt, peppercorns, and bay leaves. Cover with water and bring to a boil. Let simmer for an hour or two until the meat is tender. Skim off foam. Remove from heat; strain. The meat may be ground up and put back into the broth. Serve broth hot.

RINDFLEISCHSUPPE MIT NUDELN (BEEF SOUP WITH NOODLES)

Put some beef soup bones in a big soup pot. Cover with water and cook over a high fire. Skim off the foam and scum as it rises to the top. Add some salt, a little pepper, an onion pierced with cloves and a bay leaf. Simmer over a low fire partially covered for about 1½ hours. Take the bones from the broth and remove all meat and scoop the marrow out of the bones; add to the broth. Throw the bones away. Simmer broth. Add noodles. Cook until noodles are done. Correct seasoning if necessary. Serve hot.

OCHSENSCHWANZSUPPE (OXTAIL SOUP)

Cut oxtail into small pieces; brown in hot fat; cover with water and add some salt. Simmer for several hours. Remove meat from bones. Put the meat back into the broth. Throw away the bones. Add chopped onions, diced carrots, chopped celery, and some rice. Cover and simmer until rice is done. Skim off the fat, then add some tomatoes and simmer a little bit longer. Serve hot.

LEBERKNOEDELSUPPE (LIVER DUMPLING SOUP)

Remove membranes from liver and chop finely. Combine liver, at least one egg, some butter, bread crumbs, chopped parsley, and salt. Mix well. Let sit in a cool place for about a half

*MAN SOLL DEN TAG NICHT
VOR DEM ABEND LOBEN.*

ONE SHOULD NOT PRAISE THE DAY
BEFORE THE EVENING.

(Don't count your chickens
before they hatch.)

hour. Bring some beef broth to a boil. Form liver mixture into balls and drop into simmering broth. Cook until done. Serve the liver dumplings and broth in big soup bowls.

BOHNENSUPPE
(BEAN SOUP)

Soak navy or northern beans overnight. Put beans, a ham bone or ham hocks in a kettle, and cover with water. Cook until beans are tender. Add salt to taste.

ERBSENSUPPE
(PEA SOUP)

Soak dried split peas overnight in cold water to let them swell. In the morning, drain peas and rinse them. Put the peas in a pot with cut up pieces of ham; cover with water. If desired sliced carrots, onions, and celery may be added. Cook until peas are mushy. Season with salt to taste.

KARTOFFELSUPPE
(POTATO SOUP)

Slice potatoes and cook in boiling salted water until tender. Don't drain. Cut bacon into small pieces; fry until crisp;

remove from drippings. Fry chopped onions in bacon drippings until golden. Remove onions from drippings. Brown some flour in drippings; add some of the water in which the potatoes boiled; stir to make a thick gravy. Add this gravy, the cooked onions, and fried bacon bits to the potatoes. Mix well! If soup is too thick, add more water. Simmer a few minutes. Serve hot!

GEMUESESUPPE
(VEGETABLE SOUP)

Put beef soup bones in a big pot. Cover with water; add some salt; cook slowly for 1 to 2 hours. Remove pieces of meat from the bones. Return meat to the broth; throw away the bones. Chop whatever fresh vegetables are available or desired; add to the broth. Cook until vegetables are tender.

KOHLSUPPE
(CABBAGE SOUP)

Put some chopped bacon, pieces of potatoes, chopped cabbage, salt, and other seasoning desired in a pot. Cover with water. Cook until vegetables are done.

THE GERMAN immigrant family served these salads as side dishes at meals, yet they are quite hearty. They made fresh vegetable salads with seasonal vegetables such as small fresh green leaves of lettuce and wilted them with seasoned hot bacon fat and vinegar. Or they dressed tiny sliced cucumbers with sour cream. Carefully seasoned salads made of cooked fruits and vegetables added variety to the meal. Cooked meat salads were sometimes used as the main course for supper or as sandwich fillings.

SALAT VON GRUENEM KOHL
(GREEN CABBAGE SALAD)

Take a nice, firm head of cabbage, remove the outer leaves, and cut the cabbage into thin strips. Stir salt according to taste into the cabbage. Let the cabbage and salt stand for 1 hour. Before serving, add 1 thinly sliced onion, some pepper, about 3 tablespoons vinegar, and 4 tablespoons of bacon fat.

WARMER KRAUTSALAT
(WARM CABBAGE SALAD)

Finely slice 1/2 head of cabbage. Steam cabbage using 2 tablespoons good fat from a roast or some fresh lard and some water until done. Remove pot from the fire, and add enough vinegar to give cabbage a sour taste. Finally add 1 to 2 tablespoons sugar.

SALMON SALAT
(SALMON SALAD)

To 1 can of salmon, add some celery, 1 onion, 1 pod sweet green pepper, and a couple slices of tomato. Finely chop the vegetables; add salt, olive oil, and vinegar or the juice of a lemon.

HAERINGSALAT FUER DEN TAEGLICHEN TISCH
(HERRING SALAD FOR THE DAILY TABLE)

Remove herring from brine. Lay in fresh water. Wash them; remove skin and bone.

Cut into cubes and add boiled potatoes, canned beets, pickles, apples, a small piece of roast meat, 2 hard boiled eggs, and 1 onion. Add salt, pepper, sugar, olive oil, and vinegar as a sauce.

HUEHNER SALAT MIT GELATINE
(CHICKEN SALAD WITH GELATIN)

Cook an old hen until tender; season as desired. When cooled, cut the meat into cubes. Soften a package of gelatin for five minutes in a cup of water. Season the chicken broth with some red pepper and very thin slices of lemon; pour over gelatin. Cool, add meat and a can of drained peas. Chill overnight; in hot weather set on ice. Serve with mayonnaise.

HUEHNER SALAT
(CHICKEN SALAD)

Boil a 2½ to 3 pound chicken until tender. When it is cold, remove the meat from the bones. Chop the meat into pieces the size of peas. Chop 5 stalks of celery and mix them with the meat. Then blend together 2 hard boiled mashed egg yolks, 1 teaspoon mustard, 1 teaspoon salt, 2 teaspoons sweet oil or butter, and a dash of red pepper; add 2 finely chopped hard boiled egg whites. Mix with meat and celery. Serve garnished with celery leaves.

PECAN SALAT
(PECAN SALAD)

Take 2 cups of shelled pecans and chop them. Add 1 cup chopped celery, 2 tablespoons of sugar, 1 cup of sweet cream, and 1 teaspoon salt. Mix well. Serve with cake.

ROTE RUEBEN SALAT
(RED BEET SALAD)

Wash beets and cover with boiling water and cook until tender, then pour them in a sieve. Peel them and cut them into little pieces. Season with salt, pepper, and a little vinegar.

SCHINKENSALAT
(HAM SALAD)

Finely chop left over cooked ham, and add a finely chopped heart of a lettuce. Combine in a double boiler 1 teaspoon salt, 1 teaspoon pepper, 1 teaspoon mustard, 1/2 pint vinegar, 1 tablespoon butter, and 3 well beaten egg yolks. Cook in double boiler stirring constantly until thickened. Cool. Mix with the ham and lettuce. Finally, pour a cup of sweet cream over the salad.

BRUNNENKRESSENSALAT
(WATERCRESS SALAD)

Wash watercress well. Break into short pieces. Blend 1 hard boiled egg yolk with mustard, salt, pepper, and oil to a smooth sauce. Pour over the water cress. Garnish with quarters of hard boiled eggs.

FLEISCHSALAT
(MEAT SALAD)

Cut left over roast meat, tomatoes, and onions as finely as possible. Add vinegar, 1 teaspoon black pepper, and salt. Mix. Then add 2 tablespoons of sweet cream. This simple dish is quick to prepare. It tastes cool and refreshing on hot summer days.

EIN NEUER SALAT
(A NEW SALAD)

Combine 2 cupfuls of chopped celery, 2 oranges cut into small pieces, and 2 cups of seedless raisins which have been cut into halves. Mix 1 cup of mayonnaise with 1 cup of grated apple. Cover the celery mixture with the mayonnaise mixture. Serve on lettuce leaves cut into strips with a scissor. It's delicious!

GURKENSALAT
(CUCUMBER SALAD)

Slice half grown cucumbers for salad. Salt the cucumbers and lay them into a sieve. Let them drain. Then put them in a dish and cover them with wine vinegar so that salt is drawn out again. In the meantime lay a cloth in a sieve, pour the cucumbers on it and press them firmly; put them in a crockery or glass container with onions and ground pepper; pour cold wine vinegar over it, and finally add some oil.

BANANE UND NUSS SALAT
(BANANA AND NUT SALAD)

Combine 4 bananas cut into slices and 1 cup chopped nuts or peanuts. Cover with mayonnaise. Serve on white lettuce leaves garnished with whipped cream.

WAS VERSTEHT DER BAUER VON GURKENSALAT?

WHAT DOES THE FARMER UNDERSTAND ABOUT CUCUMBER SALAD?

(This is quite over my head.)

BOHNEN SALAT
(BEAN SALAD)

Pull the strings from green beans; wash and cut them into pieces; cook in salted water until done. Drain off water and prepare them for serving with fat, pepper, vinegar, chopped onion, and some sugar.

CELLERIE SALAT
(CELERY SALAD)

Wash the celery and cut it into small pieces. Chop 1 apple into small pieces, and chop 1 cup of pecans. Mix all of this together with a sauce made as follows: melt 1 tablespoon butter and mix with 1 tablespoon flour until smooth; add 1 cup boiling milk, about 1 tablespoon each of mustard and vinegar, and 1 teaspoon each of pepper and salt. Then add 1 beaten egg and the juice of 1 lemon.

GRUENER SALAT
(GREEN SALAD)

Remove bad outer leaves from head of lettuce. Separate lettuce leaves and wash them. Season with sugar, vinegar, some warm fat, and a little salt. One can prepare a similar salad using watercress.

KARTOFFELSALAT
(POTATO SALAD)

Wash and cook potatoes in their peels in salted water until done. Drain the water from the potatoes, pull the skins off and cut the potatoes into thin slices. The salad is then made with pepper, fat, onions, vinegar, and some boiling water. The boiling water makes the potatoes juicy.

KARTOFFELSALAT MIT SPECK
(POTATO SALAD WITH BACON)

Wash and cut potatoes in half. Cook in lightly salted water until tender when pierced with a fork; drain. Dry potatoes by shaking pan over a low fire. Peel and cut potatoes into thin slices. Fry slices of bacon. Crumble slices of fried bacon. Fry chopped onions in the bacon drippings until tender. Stir some vinegar, sugar, salt, and pepper into the onions and bacon drippings; heat mixture to boiling. Add crumbled bacon. Pour over hot potato slices and toss to coat evenly. Serve warm.

SCREIBEN SIE IHR LIEBLINGSREZEPT HIER!
WRITE YOUR FAVORITE RECIPE HERE!

_____
_____
_____
_____
_____
_____
_____
_____
_____
_____
_____
_____
_____
_____
_____
_____
_____
_____
_____
_____
_____
_____
_____
_____
_____
_____
_____
_____
_____

PASS IT ON TO THE NEXT GENERATION!

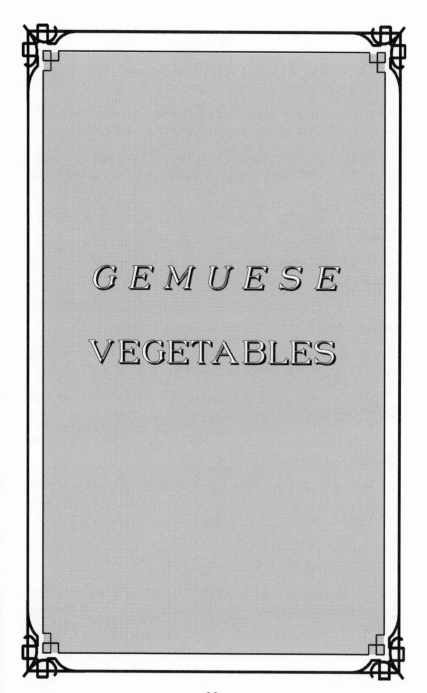

GEMUESE

VEGETABLES

"Koch Tips" From Long Ago

Add a teaspoon of lemon juice to each quart of water when cooking rice to keep the grains separate and white.

After washing, put string beans in boiling water for five minutes, then the strings can be easily pulled from the beans.

When getting ready to mash potatoes, add a teaspoon of baking powder. Beat them vigorously. They will turn out light and creamy.

Sprinkle a little flour on potatoes to be fried. They will fry to a beautiful brown.

Make cold baked potatoes fresh again by dipping them in hot water, then heat them in a moderate oven.

Boil sweet potatoes in water to which a teaspoonful of sugar has been added.

Grease the skins of sweet potatoes with lard before putting them in the oven to bake. The skins will pull off more easily.

Cook green vegetables in an uncovered pot so that their natural color is saved.

Boil cauliflower head down so that the scum will not settle on the white part.

Save time! Don't shell green peas. Wash the pods of peas well and boil them. While boiling, the pods will burst; skim them off; the peas settle to the bottom.

A teaspoon of sugar added to cooking turnips will improve their flavor and lessen their cooking oder.

The flavor and color of lima beans are better whenever a teaspoon of baking soda is added to the water in which they are cooked.

To keep a lid on a pot of boiling beans or other vegetables from boiling over, add a teaspoonful of butter to the water.

First add salt to the water, and spinach will not have to be washed anywhere near as much as usual.

Use a small brush to remove silks from an ear of orn.

BEFORE COOKING, fresh garden vegetables were picked over and thoroughly washed, green string beans were snapped and the strings pulled off; potatoes peeled; peas shelled; and corn kernels cut off the cob. Most cooks of that era believed in cooking vegetables in large amounts of salted water until they were very tender. Seasoning usually consisted of pieces of bacon, ham, or butter and some salt and pepper. They ladled the vegetables into bowls and set them along with other foods in front of family and friends. Everyone sat at a long rectangular wooden table with a bench on at least one side for children.

GEKOCHTE GRUENE BOHNEN
(COOKED GREEN BEANS)

Pull the strings from green beans, then cut them in half. Cook in salted water until done. Drain the water from the beans. Add sweet cream, pepper, some sugar, and 1 onion.

—or—

Wash the green beans and put them in cold water with some baking soda before setting pot on the fire to cook. If rain water is used, baking soda isn't necessary. Instead, cover them with hot water and cook until done. Season them with fat, salt, pepper, and a little sugar.

GEKOCHTE GRUENE BOHNEN MIT RAHM
(COOKED GREEN BEANS WITH CREAM)

Cook washed and cut green beans in salted water until done. Pour off the water; add chopped parsley and cream blended with flour. For ¼ quart beans, take 1 tablespoon of cream and flour. Toss the beans with creamed mixture. Bring to boil. Serve.

GEKOCHTE ROTE RUEBEN
(COOKED RED BEETS)

Wash beets and cook them in salted water until done. Pour off the water and peel the beets. Cut the beets into pieces. Season with vinegar, sugar, and pepper.

GEKOCHTER KOHL
(COOKED CABBAGE)

Cut a large head of cabbage into quarters and steam in a lot of boiling salted water until the core is soft. Drain. Melt a piece of butter the size of an egg, stir 2 tablespoons flour into the butter, add 1½ cups meat broth or water. Add the drained cabbage. Put a lid on the pot, and stew for a few minutes without stirring so that the pieces will not fall apart.

—or—

Remove all dirty leaves. Wash, clean, and quarter the head of cabbage. Cook it in water with some salt until done. Pour the water off. Season the cabbage with fat, pepper, a little vinegar, and, if necessary, some salt.

GEBACKNER KOHL
(BAKED CABBAGE)

Cut 1 head of cabbage into 4 parts and cook in water until soft. Drain water from cabbage and chop fine. Add 2 tablespoons of butter, ½ cup cream, 2 eggs, salt and pepper. Stir well. Bake for half-an-hour.

—or—

Take one gallon cabbage, ½ pint vinegar, 1 pint sour cream, ½ cup sugar, 1 teaspoon flour, 2 eggs, and 1 teaspoon each of salt, pepper, and mustard. Chop the cabbage finely; sprinkle with salt, pepper and mustard. Combine vinegar, sugar, and some butter in a pan; bring to a boil. Add beaten eggs, cream, and flour. Bring to a boil; pour over the cabbage.

KOHL MIT AEPFELN
(CABBAGE WITH APPLES)

Finely cut cabbage. Cook it with water, butter, and, if necessary, salt. Cut apples into 6 to 8 pieces. Combine. Let everything cook well.

ROTKOHL MIT ESSIG
(RED CABBAGE WITH VINEGAR)

For 3 pints of finely cut cabbage, use 2 tablespoons of meat drippings, 1 teaspoon salt, a knife tip of pepper, 1/2 teaspoon caraway seeds, 2 tablespoons of sugar, and 1 cup of water. Stew until done. Ten minutes before serving add 1/2 cup of not too strong vinegar. White cabbage fixed in this way tastes just as good.

WEISSKOHL MIT MILCHSOSSE
(WHITE CABBAGE WITH MILK SAUCE)

Cover 1 average sized finely cut head of cabbage with boiling salted water; cook until done. Just before serving, combine 1 cup milk, 1 tablespoon butter, 1 tablespoon flour, 1 egg yolk, and some salt in a pan; stir over a low fire until it's creamy. Drain cabbage; put in a bowl; pour sauce over it.

BLUMENKOHL
(CAULIFLOWER)

Clean a head of cauliflower leaving it as big as possible. Cook it in salted water until soft; carefully take it out of the water; drain. In the meantime, heat 1/2 liter cream and 1 piece of butter. Add 1 cup cold cream, 3 to 4 egg yolks, some spoons of flour and salt to the mixture and beat. Put it on the fire. Beat continually until thick. Do not boil sauce. Pour over cauliflower; sprinkle with nutmeg.

—or—

Break cauliflower into pieces; cook in salted water until soft. Combine 1 tablespoon melted butter and 1 tablespoon flour; add 1 cup milk, some salt, and a little vinegar.

—or—

Pull stems off a head of cauliflower; use a pointed knife to get the little leaves out, but leave the head as whole as possible. Put the cauliflower in water, so if by chance, a worm is hiding in the cauliflower, it will come out. Cook the cauliflower in boiling water until tender. Remove from water carefully with a skimming spoon. Pour a thick cream sauce over it.

—or—

Handle cauliflower carefully so that it won't break. Bundle it in a clean white cloth, and cook it until done in lightly salted water. Remove from water. Drain. Remove cloth. Pour a sauce over the cooked cauliflower made of melted butter, pepper, some peppercorns, and some corn starch.

GEKOCHTE MOHRRUEBEN
(COOKED CARROTS)

Wash, scrape, and cut carrots into thin strips; cook them in water until done. Add sugar, butter, salt, a little pepper, some vinegar, and corn starch.

GRUENES CORN
(FRESH CORN)

Cut corn from the cob. Put it in a pot with a mixture of 1/2 milk and 1/2 water. Cook until soft. Add some salt and about 2 spoons of butter. Blend a piece of butter with flour and add to the corn; cook until it is smooth.

—or—

Cut young corn from cobs. Wash it, and cook it with a little salt and water until done. Add butter.

> ## WER DEN PFENNIG NICHT EHRT, IST DES TALERS NICHT WERT.
> (Take care of the pennies, and the dollars will take care of themselves.)

EIERPFLANZE
(EGGPLANT)

Take 1 big eggplant and peel it; cook in salted water. When it's done, drain in a sieve. Add 1 1/2 cups fine bread crumbs, 4 beaten eggs, salt, pepper, and some butter. Grease a mold with butter, and pour the mixture into it. Bake in oven until brown.

—or—

Cut the eggplant into thin slices. Let sit in a strong salt water solution for several hours, so that the characteristic bitter taste of the eggplant is drawn out. Take a big tablespoon of butter and heat it in a frying pan. Dip the eggplant slices in a beaten egg and roll in cracker crumbs. These are fried on both sides until nicely browned. They must be thoroughly cooked.

—or—

Pare the eggplant, cut into slices, and put them into salt water for an hour. Remove slices from the salt water and dry them. Sprinkle with salt and fry them in hot lard until brown.

GEKOCHTER KOHLRABI
(COOKED KOHLRABI)

Peel, wash, and cut kohlrabi into thin slices or little strips; cook it in water until done. Then prepare it for the table with butter, pepper, salt, and corn starch.

DIE FLINTE INS KORN WERFEN.
TO THROW ONE'S GUN INTO THE CORNFIELD.
(To lose courage; to give up.)

GOMBO
(GUMBO)

Peel and cut onion into little pieces and saute in a little fat for a few minutes. Add peeled and cut up tomatoes; cook about 15 minutes. Add okra cut into 1 inch long pieces. Season with salt and pepper, and cook for about 1 hour.

—or—

Combine 1 quart okra, 3 tomatoes, 1 little piece of chopped onion, 1/4 cup vinegar, 1 little piece of butter, salt, and pepper. Cook until it is soft.

OKRA
(OKRA)

Cut the ends and tips from quite young pods of okra. Add salt. Pour hot boiling water over the okra, and cook quickly on a hot stove. Drain the water; let the okra cool. Then add 4 table-spoons of vinegar, 1 to 2 slices of chopped onions, and some salt. This makes 1 quart okra.

GEKOCHTER GRUENE ERBSEN
(COOKED GREEN PEAS)

Carefully pick over peas because little worms like to hide in them. Wash peas and cook until done. Then prepare them with salt, fat, some sugar, and corn starch.

—or—

Wash peas and put them into cold water with some baking soda. Cook until done. If rainwater is used, baking soda is not necessary. Instead pour hot water over the peas, and cook them until done. Season with lard, salt, chopped parsley, a little sugar, and a chopped onion (optional).

ERBSEN UND SPECK
(PEAS AND BACON)

In a pot, fry 6 slices of bacon until they are brown, but not dry. Then pour all but three tablespoons fat out of the pot. In this fat, fry one finely chopped onion until brown. Empty a can of peas into it; add some salt and pepper. Stir gently until very hot. Before the peas are served, stir in four tablespoons of whipped cream. Garnish with the 6 strips of fried bacon.

GEBACKENE KARTOFFELKUGELN
(BAKED POTATO BALLS)

Peel and grate a plateful of boiled potatoes which have been cooked the day before. Make potatoes into a dough on a noodle board using three eggs, salt, and some pepper; add flour until the dough is quite stiff. Form into balls the size of big walnuts. Brush with beaten egg whites and roll in bread crumbs. Fry in extremely hot lard. Add to soup or to a sauce.

KARTOFFELKLOESSE AUF DEUTSCHE
ART ZUBEREITET
(GERMAN STYLE POTATO DUMPLINGS)

Take 1 cup of mashed potatoes, and add two eggs, ½ cup milk,

> ## DEM DUEMMSTEN BAUERN WACHSEN DIE
> ## GROESSTEN KAROFFELN.
> ## THE DUMBEST FARMERS GROW
> ## THE BIGGEST POTATOES.
> ## (Fools have fortune.)

and as much flour as needed to make the mixture quite stiff. Drop by spoonfuls into boiling salted water. Cook for 1/4 hour. These potato dumplings go really well with veal or pork roasts which have a rich sauce.

GEBRATENE KARTOFFELN
(FRIED POTATOES)

Wash and peel potatoes; slice very thin. Let them sit in cold water long enough to remove a part of the starch. Dry. Fry in hot lard a few pieces at a time. The lard must be boiling hot. As soon as the potatoes are golden brown, remove them from the fat and drain them in a sieve.

KARTOFFEL-KRAPFEN
(POTATO FRITTERS)

Combine 3 1/2 cups of flour, 2 eggs, 1 cup sugar, 3 teaspoons of baking powder, 1 cup cooked, mashed potatoes, and 3/4 cup of milk or more if necessary. Form into the desired size and shape. The fat in which the fritters will be fried must be quite hot.

KARTOFFELGERICHT
(POTATO DISH)

Cook potatoes until done, then drain. Dry by shaking them in a pan over the fire. Add milk, butter, and salt. All of this is mashed with a potato masher and mixed well. Put the mixture on a pie plate; put in oven to brown.

GEBACKENE KARTOFFELN
(BAKED POTATOES)

Crush cooked potatoes; mix in 3 to 4 beaten eggs, and a piece

---

MEIN HAUS, MEINE WELT.
MY HOUSE, MY WORLD.
(My home is my castle.)

of butter the size of a hen egg. Add some sweet milk, salt, and pepper as desired. Bake until brown.

GEKOCHTE KARTOFFELN
(BOILED POTATOES)

Wash potatoes and peel thinly removing all sprouts and blemishes. Put them in cold water and wash them again. Cut large potatoes in halves or quarters. Place in pot; put in just enough water to cover potatoes. Add salt; boil until potatoes are done; drain. Let them stand for a little while in an uncovered pot over good heat, shaking frequently to let the steam escape. Save the water in which the potatoes were cooked for soups.

BRATKARTOFFELN
(FRIED POTATOES)

Wash potatoes thoroughly and boil in their skins. Peel them as soon as they are done. When cold, slice, then fry with finely chopped onion in hot fat until browned. Sprinkle with salt. leftover boiled potatoes may be used.

KARTOFFELN MIT BUTTER
(POTATOES WITH BUTTER)

Peel potatoes and wash them, then put in a pot with cold water and a little handful of salt; set them on the stove to cook. When the potatoes are soft, drain the water off. Then add 1 to 2 tablespoons of butter and some chopped parsley. Simmer a bit on the stove.

GEWUERFELTE KARTOFFELN MIT EIERN
(CUBED POTATOES WITH EGGS)

After boiling, cut potatoes into cubes. Put cubes in a casserole with a piece of butter; shake several times; pour some well beaten eggs over the potatoes. Cook until done. Serve with beef.

GEBACKENE SUESSKARTOFFELN
(BAKED SWEET POTATOES)

Scrub average sized sweet potatoes. Dry them. Lay them with their peelings on in a hot oven. When soft, serve immediately.

EIN BILLIGES GEMUESE
(A CHEAP VEGETABLE)

Cut a big onion into little cubes. Take a plateful of potatoes and a plateful of pumpkins; cut into little cubes, add a good spoonful of butter, pepper, and salt. Cook this in a little water for 1/2 hour until done.

GLEICH UND GLEICH GESELLT SICH GERN.

LIKE AND ALIKE LIKE TO ASSOCIATE.

(Birds of a feather flock together.)

GEDAEMPFTER KUERBIS
(STEAMED PUMPKIN)

Cut a pumpkin into halves. Remove inner fibers and seeds. Rub each cavity with salt, butter, and some sugar. Place in a roasting pan. Steam it in a not too hot oven until light brown.

GEKOCHTER KUERBIS
(COOKED PUMPKIN)

Peel a pumpkin, cut into small pieces, and cook in water with salt until done. Prepare it with salt, pepper, sugar, butter, and corn starch.

GEBACKENER KUERBIS
(BAKED PUMPKIN)

Cut peeled pumpkin into cubes, cook in salted water until soft. Drain in sieve. Mash pumpkin, and beat in 1 cup cream, 1 tablespoon flour, 1 finely chopped onion, salt, and pepper. Grease a mold generously with butter. Pour ½ of the pumpkin mixture into the mold. Lay finely sliced ham on top of it. Pour the remainder of the pumpkin mixture gently over the ham. Sprinkle liberally with Parmesan cheese and bread crumbs. Bake in moderate oven for thirty minutes.

GEBACKENER REIS
(BAKED RICE)

Wash rice, and cook it in water until half done. Then add milk, some salt, and sugar. Cook mixture until done. When the rice is cooled, add 2 egg yolks and vanilla. Stir well. Beat 2 eggs whites until stiff and add sugar. Cover the rice with the stiffly beaten egg whites. Put the mixture in the oven to bake until egg whites are a light brown.

REIS AUF AMERIKANISCHE ART
(RICE AMERICAN STYLE)

Roast 1 cup rice in 3 tablespoons lard until light brown. Add finely cut onion and 2 to 3 slices of chopped tomatoes. Beat and add some spoons of broth. Cover and let steam until rice is done. Thin noodles may be prepared in the same way.

SUESSER REIS
(SWEET RICE)

Put one cup long grain rice and 5 to 6 cups of milk in a double boiler. Cook slowly about 1¼ to 1½ hours or until rice is almost done. Add ⅔ to ¾ cup sugar and ½ teaspoon salt; cook about 30 minutes longer. Serve either hot or cold. May be sprinkled with sugar and cinnamon.

KAROFFELBAUCH.
POTATO BELLY.
(Pot Belly.)

SPINAT
(SPINACH)

Put spinach in boiling water with an onion, some baking soda, and parsley. When cooked soft, drain well; chop fine. Add salt, pepper, 2 eggs, and 1½ cups cracker crumbs. Form into a ball. Put into a cloth smeared with butter. Tie cloth, but not too tight. Put a plate into a pot, lay the cloth wrapped ball of spinach on it, and cook it in boiling water until done.

TOMATEN MIT ZUCKER
(TOMATOES WITH SUGAR)

Pull skins off 12 nice ripe tomatoes. If the peelings are hard to get off, pour boiling water over the tomatoes. Make sure they have been put in a sieve, so that the hot water doesn't stay on the tomatoes too long—otherwise they lose their good taste. When the peelings have been pulled off, cut them in thin slices and sprinkle 1 cup of sugar over them.

ROHE TOMATEN
(RAW TOMATOES)

Pour boiling water over the tomatoes to pull the peelings off. Let them cool, preferably on ice; cut them into not too thin slices; pour sugar and a little vinegar over them.

TOMATEN MIT OKRA
(TOMATOES WITH OKRA)

Fry finely cut onions in a spoon of butter until done, but not brown. Add 2 cups finely cut okra. After an hour, add 3 cups finely cut tomatoes. Let cook until everything is well done. Then mix in 1 to 2 tablespoons of flour and some butter. Add salt, sugar, and vinegar to taste. Stir this into the vegetables. Let boil thoroughly.

TOMATEN MIT KRAUT
(TOMATOES WITH CABBAGE)

Cook 1 quart tomatoes, then put them through a sieve to remove the seeds and pulp. Finely cut 2 quarts of white cabbage. Add to the tomato juice and cook in a covered kettle until done. Melt 1 big tablespoon of butter, add 2 tablespoons of flour, 2 tablespoons of onions chopped fine, and 1/4 teaspoon paprika; mix everything well. Add it to the cabbage. Salt to taste. When ready to serve, add 1 cup of thick sour cream. It's tasty and nourishing.

WEISSE RUEBEN
(TURNIPS)

Wash the turnips nice and clean. Peel them and cut into little strips; cook in water until done. Then prepare them with butter, pepper, salt, some sugar, and a little cornstarch.

WENN DIE KATZE NICHT ZU HAUSE IST,
TANZEN DIE MAEUSE.
(When the cat's away,
the mice will play.)

SCREIBEN SIE IHR LIEBLINGSREZEPT HIER!
WRITE YOUR FAVORITE RECIPE HERE!

_____
_____
_____
_____
_____
_____
_____
_____
_____
_____
_____
_____
_____
_____
_____
_____
_____
_____
_____
_____
_____
_____
_____
_____
_____
_____
_____
_____

PASS IT ON TO THE NEXT GENERATION!

BROT

BREAD

"Koch Tips" From Long Ago

If the oven is too hot when baking bread and the loaves brown on top before the bread is baked, set a pan of boiling water on the grate. The steam will keep the bread from scorching while the heat thoroughly bakes the rest of the loaf.

For greasing bread pans, it's best to use lard. Butter burns too quickly.

To glaze bread or rolls, apply freshly beaten eggs to the tops with a cloth or a soft brush before placing them in oven. If a sweet taste is preferred, a little sugar can be added to the eggs.

To freshen stale bread, wrap the loaf in a wet cloth for a minute or so, then heat in the oven for 15 to 30 minutes.

It is much easier to cut thin slices of bread for sandwiches, if the bread is a day old.

If you don't want to cut yourself, never cut bread by holding the loaf and cutting toward yourself.

To cut very fresh bread, heat knife with a thin blade over a fire, or put it in boiling water for a few minutes. Dry the knife, and it will cut very thin slices.

Baking powder biscuits will turn out much better if the dough is rolled out thinner than usual; cut out biscuits, then stack two biscuits together to bake.

Drain fried doughnuts by standing them in a shallow pan lined with tissue paper.

Don't wash a flour sieve in soapy water. Instead use bicarbonate of soda in the water; it will not stick to the fine mesh like soap does.

Dough rises better in crockery or earthware bowls, because they hold their tempeterature more evenly.

For freshening muffins, biscuits and rolls sprinkle them lightly with water, place them in one pan, and put it into another pan containing water. Heat in the oven for a few minutes. They will be as fresh as when first baked.

Potato water makes the yeast work better, and it keeps the bread moister longer.

DAS BACKEN EINFACHER MACHEN (MAKING BAKING SIMPLER)

Thick slices of home baked yeast bread or corn bread, along with freshly churned butter, were staples at meal times. *Butterbrot,* an especially thick slice of bread and butter eaten between meals, was a great snack. They purchased the white wheat flour to bake yeast breads. Corn meal was both to make yeast cakes (the leavening agent for white bread) and corn bread as well. The corn meal usually came from the settler's own corn, dried, and carried to the grist meal where it was ground.

Yeast Breads

All ingredients needed to bake bread must be at room temperature. Use a good grade of bread flour or flour especially milled using such traditional techniques as stone grinding. These flours are sometimes available in specialty stores. The German settlers scalded liquid before using it, because doing so killed any harmful bacteria which might cause the bread to sour or retard the growth of the yeast.

- Dissolve yeast in about ¼ cup of lukewarm water in a bowl.
- In another bowl, add lard or butter, sugar, and salt to the remaining liquid.
- Combine the two mixtures. Stir flour slowly into the liquid, adding enough flour to make a smooth, thick dough.

- Toss the dough onto a floured board and knead until it's smooth and elastic.
- Put the dough into a large greased bowl, and cover it with a damp cloth. Put it to rise in a warm, draft-free place.
- When its bulk has doubled again, punch it down once more, and shape into loaves.
- Put shaped dough into greased bread pans, grease tops of loaves, and cover. Shaped loaves should fill about half the bread pans.
- Let the loaves double in size.
- Put them into a pre-heated 350 to 400 degree oven to bake for about 40 minutes.

Quick Breads

Biscuits: The trick to making good biscuits is to use a soft, almost sticky, dough which has been handled as little as possible. Bake them in a preheated 400-450 degree oven for 12 to 15 minutes. Biscuits that don't touch each other in the baking pan will be lighter than those placed together.

- Put dry ingredients into a mixing bowl.
- Add shortening to the dry ingredients.
- Work the shortening into the dry ingredients with finger tips, pastry blender, or two knives, until the mixture is like coarse corn meal.
- Slowly add milk to the mixture. Blend the two together with a spoon to form a soft dough.
- Put the dough on a floured board. Work it until just smooth, then roll or pat it to a thickness of 1/2 to 1 inch thickness.
- Cut out biscuits.

Muffins: Good muffins have several secrets. Don't stir the batter until it's smooth; good muffin batter should be lumpy. Muffins like a hot (400 to 425) preheated oven. It takes about 15 to 25 minutes for the crust to turn a golden brown.
- Put all dry ingredients into a mixing bowl.

- Beat eggs in a separate bowl.
- Combine beaten eggs, melted shortening, and milk.
- Quickly stir the liquid mixture into the dry ingrdients to form a lumpy batter.
- Fill greased muffin pans no more than ½ full.

Corn Bread: *Maisbrot*, a new bread to the early German settlers, is really quite simple to prepare. It bakes in about thirty minutes or less in a 400 to 425 degree oven. The crispy bottom crust, prized by some connoisseurs, is achieved by greasing the baking pan with shortening, baking drippings, butter, or lard. Put the greased pan into the oven until it sizzles. If crispy crust is not desired, bake batter in an unheated greased pan.

- Put all dry ingredients into a mixing bowl.
- Beat eggs in a separate bowl; combine with other liquids.
- With a few quick stirs of a spoon, blend dry ingredients and egg mixture together. Don't be concerned about leaving a few lumps in the batter.
- Pour batter into preheated pan.
- Bake in a preheated oven.

Pancakes: The first step in making pancakes is to heat the griddle. Prepare the cooking surface by greasing it, and then heating it. Often more grease has to be added before a batch of pancakes can be cooked. Today's cooks don't grease the griddle. Test the heat by dropping a few drops of water on the griddle. If they dance and sputter, it's hot enough to bake pancakes.

- Put all dry ingredients into a mixing bowl.
- Slightly beat eggs and combine with other liquids.
- Make a hole in the center of the dry ingredients.
- Pour liquid mixture into it.
- Stir together until blended.
- Drop spoonfuls of batter on griddle to bake.

EIN GUTES REZEPT FUER HEFE
(A GOOD RECIPE FOR YEAST)

Bring 1 quart buttermilk to boil while continuously stirring. Add enough corn meal to make a stiff dough. When cool, add 1 yeast cake. Let it rise. Form yeast cakes. Let dry.

—or—

Shell 2 ears good, dry corn. Wash corn kernels in cold water, then pour 1½ quarts of boiling water over it, and cook until the corn is soft. More water may be needed during boiling. Let the water and corn cool until you can comfortably hold a finger in it. Pour the water in a big pan. Discard the cooked corn kernels. One must make the yeast cakes on the day that bread is to be baked, so that one can take about a pint of bread dough to mix with cornmeal and the corn water. Use enough cornmeal to make a dough stiff enough to form cakes with hands. This yields about 21 yeast cakes, let it dry in the air. It's best to wrap them in paper. When yeast cakes made in this way are used, good bread is always the result.

—or—

Dissolve 1 cake of yeast in a pint of warm water, add 1 tablespoon corn meal, 1 teaspoon salt, and 1 tablespoon of sugar. Let this mixture stand overnight to work. In the morning, slowly heat 1 pint buttermilk. Blend 1 cup flour with enough water to make a stiff dough. Add to the buttermilk and mix until smooth. Cool. Mix the yeast mixture and the buttermilk mixture. Add enough cornmeal to make a stiff dough. Form into cakes. Let dry in the shade. Turn often.

EINFACHES BROT
(SIMPLE BREAD)
Dissolve 1 big yeast cake in 1 quart luke-warm water; add some salt. Then make a stiff dough with flour. Knead until smooth and elastic. Place the dough in a greased bowl, and let it stand

> ## BROTLOS WERDEN.
> ## TO BE WITHOUT BREAD.
> ## (To lose one's livelihood.)

in a warm place to rise. In the winter, let it stand over night. After the dough has risen, knead it again. Shape into loaves and let loaves rise. Bake in a hot oven for an hour.

—or—

Soak 1 cake of yeast in ½ cup of lukewarm water. Let it stand for a few minutes, then add 2 tablespoons each of sugar, salt, and lard. Mix in 3 cups of lukewarm water; add enough flour to keep dough from sticking to hands when kneading. Knead until smooth and elastic. Form dough into a ball and put it into a greased bowl. Cover it with a damp cloth, then set it in a warm place until it has doubled in size. Punch dough down and knead it again. Divide it into loaves and put the loaves in greased pans. Cover loaves with a damp cloth again and let rise until double in bulk. Bake in a hot oven for first 15 minutes or so, then bake in a moderate oven until done.

DEUTSCHE STOLLEN
(GERMAN STOLLEN)

For 3 quarts flour take 1 pound butter, 6 to 8 eggs, 1 package seedless raisins, 1 cup of well cleaned currants, 1 tablespoon of cardamom seeds, 1 teaspoon ground cloves, sugar to make the dough taste sweet, 2½ dissolved yeast cakes (make dough with fresh yeast cakes), some salt, and as much milk as it takes to make the dough stiff like bread dough. All ingredients must be warm, especially in the winter. Thoroughly knead the dough. Let it sit in warm oven over night to rise. The next morning, knead dough again. Put in bread pans to rise. Bake. When done, spread tops with butter, sprinkle with powdered sugar and cinnamon. Whoever likes a lot of seasoning may add a piece of candied lemon peel and some finely chopped nuts.

BACKPULVER BISCUITS
(BAKING POWDER BISCUITS)

Use 2 pints of flour, 1 piece of butter the size of an egg, 3 heaping teaspoons of baking powder, a pinch of salt, sweet milk, or cream.

—or—

Take 3½ cups flour, 3 teaspoons baking powder, 1 cupful of butter or lard. Stir the baking powder into the flour and sift. Blend butter into flour mixture. Add enough milk to make a light dough. Shape into biscuits and bake in a hot oven.

SUEDNERBISCUITS
(SOUTHERN BISCUITS)

Combine 1 cup flour to 1 spoonful of fat; mix with warm milk and roll out; cut with biscuit cutter; bake 10 minutes in a hot oven.

RAHMKRAENZEL
(CREAM CROWN)

Sift one pound flour in a pan. Cut ¾ pound butter into the flour. Make a well into the mixture; put 10 tablespoons thick sour cream in it; mix quickly into a light dough. Make a crown of the dough. Brush it with a beaten egg. Bake in a hot oven.

FRUEHSTUECK GEMS
(BREAKFAST GEMS)

Pour 1½ cups sour milk over 2 cups oatmeal and let soak overnight. Then add ½ cup molasses, 1 teaspoon soda, 1 teaspoon salt, 2 eggs, 1 tablespoon clarified butter, and 1 cup flour. Mix well and put dough into muffin tins; bake in hot oven.

MUFFINS
(MUFFINS)

Mix 3 eggs, 1 teaspoon baking powder, 1 cup milk, and some salt; make it stiff with flour, so that one can put the dough with a tablespoon into smooth or fluted muffin pans. Put a knife tip of butter on each muffin; bake in a hot oven. These muffins taste almost like bread.

EIN EI MUFFINS
(ONE EGG MUFFINS)

Sift 2 cups flour, 2 teaspoons baking powder, a scant teaspoon of salt, and ¼ cup sugar three times. Then cut in ¼ cup butter or lard. Add 1 egg and 1 cup milk; beat well. This yields 8 excellent muffins.

BISCHOFSBROT
(BISHOP'S BREAD)

Beat well 2 eggs and ¾ cup sugar together. Add ½ cup sliced almonds, ½ cup raisins, and enough flour to make a firm dough. Bake in a flat pan. When it's done cut in long thin pieces. Then bake all pieces until golden.

PFEFFERKUCHEN
(GINGER BREAD)

Use the following ingredients to bake this bread: 1 cup sugar, ½ cup fat, 1 cup sour milk, 1 cup molasses, 3 eggs, ½ teaspoon soda, 3 teaspoons ginger, some salt, and about 3 cups flour (more or less). Bake in a bread pan.

ZWIEBELKUCHEN
(ONION CAKE)

With your hands, rub together 1½ cups flour, ½ cup lard, ½ cup baking powder, and some salt. Add as much water or milk as is needed to make a dough that can be rolled out in thin sheets. Lay dough in round pans. Finely chop 4—not too big—onions, and saute with butter, a pinch of salt, and some water until soft. Then take them off the fire, and add 1 cup of sour cream to the onions. Pour it over the dough, and let it bake in the oven until done.

DEUTSCHER EIERKUCHEN
(GERMAN EGG PANCAKE)

Mix 4 egg yolks, 6 tablespoons flour, ¼ quart sour cream, and some salt. Add ¼ quart sweet milk. Just before baking, add 6 stiffly beaten egg whites. This is enough for three cakes.

KARTOFFELPFANNKUCHEN
(POTATO PANCAKES)

Mix 1 cup grated potatoes, 2 eggs, salt, 2 cups milk (half water and half milk may be used), and 1 cup flour. Brown on both sides.

—or—

Grind two raw potatoes in a meat grinder. Add 3 eggs, some salt, and a little flour. Form into little cakes and fry in fat until brown.

UM DAS LIEBE BROT ARBEITEN.

TO WORK FOR DEAR BREAD.

(To work for the bare necessities.)

PFANNKUCHEN
(PANCAKES)

Mix milk, 2 eggs, some salt, and as much flour as needed to make a thin dough. Brown on both sides in very hot fat.

TOASTBROT
(TOAST BREAD)

Take some old dried bread and cut into pieces. Dip the pieces in beaten eggs. Bake them on a greased cookie sheet until they are brown. Lay them on a plate and sprinkle with sugar and some lemon juice. Serve hot.

ZWIEBACK
(ZWIEBACK)

When baking bread, set aside 2 to 3 pounds of dough. To this dough, add 5 to 6 eggs, ½ pound lard or butter, ½ pound brown sugar, and enough flour to make the dough as stiff as bread dough. Put in a warm place to rise. Punch down. Shape dough into balls about the size of an egg. Make an indentation in the middle of each ball. Lay balls in a pan; let rise about 1 inch. Place the yolk of an egg and some sugar in each ball. Bake.

BUTTER GEBACKENES
(BUTTER PASTRY)

Take 4 eggs, 2 cups sugar, ¾ cup butter, ½ cup water, ½ teaspoon soda, and mix to a dough. Roll out the dough. Fry pieces of the dough in hot fat.

> ## KALTE HAENDE, WARMES HERZ.
> ### (Cold hands, warm heart.)

SEHR GUTES MAISBROT
(VERY GOOD CORN BREAD)

Sift together 1 cup corn meal and 1 cup wheat flour; add 2 teaspoons baking powder and a pinch of salt. Stir in 1 egg, 1 cup milk and 2 tablespoons lard. Pour into hot greased pan and bake in a hot oven.

MAISKUCHEN ZUM FRUEHSTUECK
(CORN CAKES FOR BREAKFAST)

Mix 3 eggs, 1/2 cup milk, 1 teaspoon salt, and 1 tablespoon sugar. Add a mixture of 1/2 corn meal and 1/2 flour and 1 spoon of baking powder to make a light dough. Drop by spoonfuls into hot fat to fry until done.

GUTER BOEHMISCHER SEMMELN
(GOOD BOHEMIAN ROLLS)

For every egg used, take 1/2 ounce sugar and 1/2 ounce of very fine white bread crumbs. Beat egg yolks and sugar with a whisk, and combine with the juice and the grated outer skin of 1 lemon; beat for about 1/4 hour. Sprinkle mixture with the fine white bread crumbs. Fold this mixture into stiffly beaten egg whites. Pour into well greased baking tins. Bake 1 hour. For 6 persons, 8 eggs will be sufficient.

SCHMALZKUCHEN
(SHORT CAKE)

Use about 1 cup sugar, 1 cup sweet milk, 2 eggs, 1 1/2 teaspoons baking power, 4 tablespoons of melted fat, 1 teaspoon salt, and enough flour to make as soft a dough as possible which can still be rolled out. Cut any kind of figures out of dough; fry in fat until done. Sprinkle sugar over them.

FETTKUCHEN
(DOUGHNUTS)

Take 3 eggs, 1 cup sugar, 1/2 cup milk, 1 tablespoon butter, some lemon, 2 tablespoons baking powder, and enough flour to make a soft dough. Roll it out. Form rings. Fry!

FETTKRAPFEN
(FRITTERS)

Take 1 cup sugar, 4 tablespoons butter, 3 eggs, 1 cup milk, 3 tablespoons baking powder, and enough flour so that the dough is easy to roll out. Cut out into the desired shapes. Cook in hot fat.

—or—

Take 1 1/2 cups sugar, 1 cup sour milk, 1/2 cup butter, some salt, 1 teaspoon soda, and enough flour to make dough that rolls out. Drop pieces in hot fat; cook until browned.

NORWEGISCHER FRUEHSTUECKSKUCHEN
(NORWEGIAN BREAKFAST CAKE)

Beat together 4 eggs and 4 tablespoonfuls of sugar in a bowl. Then add 1 1/2 cups of sweet cream, 1 teaspoonful of salt, and enough flour to roll out. Then cut the dough into squares. Have ready a pan 1/2 full of hot fat. Put squares of dough into hot fat to cook. They should seethe quickly. Be careful when taking squares from the pan so that they don't break. If one would like to have them real nice, roll them in powdered sugar.

DIE LIEBE GEHT DURCH DEN MAGEN.
(The way to a man's heart is
through his stomach.)

SCREIBEN SIE IHR
LIEBLINGSREZEPT HIER!
WRITE YOUR FAVORITE RECIPE HERE!

PASS IT ON TO THE NEXT GENERATION!

KUCHEN

CAKE

"Koch Tips" From Long Ago

A good way to separate egg whites from yolks is to break them into a funnel; the whites slide through the tube of the funnel, leaving the yolk behind.

Cover egg yolks with water. They'll keep for several days.

Never soak an egg beater. And never let the cogs get wet.

When mixing cake batter, use a big wooden spoon; it makes a better cake.

Use a little hot milk to make creaming butter and sugar for cakes easier.

To keep raisins or nuts from sinking to the bottom of a cake, heat them in the oven, then stir them gently into the batter just before putting the cake in the oven to bake.

Freshen coconut by soaking it in fresh milk a little while before using it.

Put a whole fresh coconut in the oven for a few minutes to make it easier to break open.

To get a baked cake out of its pan more easily, set it on a cold damp cloth as soon as it's taken from the oven for a minute or so.

One cup of molasses will give just as much sweetness as one cup of sugar.

Butter is the first choice for most cooks, because of its good flavor, but any fat that has a mild flavor may be used to bake a cake.

Always sift flour before measuring.

Dip a stale cake in cold, sweet milk for just a second, then put it in a moderate oven to freshen it.

Always put pieces of fresh apples in a cake tin to keep the cake fresh.

To keep the icing from running off the cake, dust a little flour or cornstarch over it before frosting it.

Frost the bottom crust of a cake because it's usually more level and softer than the top crust.

DAS BACKEN EINFACHER MACHEN (MAKING BAKING SIMPLER)

Home baked cakes may best be described as having love as their main ingredient. Custom required that more than one cake be offered for the afternoon *Kaffee und Kuchen*. Guests sat around a table covered by the best cloth and set with the best dishes and flatware. They felt as if they were royalty. A compliment to the hostess on the delicious cake brought pleasure to her heart as nothing else could.

Butter Cakes: These cakes require butter or other shortening. While butter is preferred, real white cakes must be made with a white shortening. Good cakes require the best and freshest ingredients available at room temperature. When getting ready to bake a cake, assemble all needed ingredients, and preheat the oven.

The pans must be prepared before mixing the cake batter. They may be lightly greased and then dusted with flour, or the bottom of the pan may be fitted with heavy paper. Clean brown paper, white wrapping paper, or waxed paper work well.

Some butter cakes call for the egg yolks and whites to be separated. Beat the yolks and add them to the creamed shortening and sugar. Egg whites are beaten until stiff and then folded into the batter after all other ingredients have been mixed into it.

These cakes need a 325 to 375 degree oven. The German immigrant cook stuck a straw in the cake to check if it was done. If it came out clean, then the cake was done. A wooden toothpick will do the same job today. A cake that is ready to take from the oven should be just brown and have begun to shrink from the sides of the pan.

- Cream butter or other shortening.
- Gradually add sugar to creamed shortening, beat until light.
- Combine dry ingredients.
- Combine milk and flavoring.
- Add alternately milk mixture with dry ingredients to creamed mixture.
- Pour batter into prepared pans to bake.

WER ZULETZT LACHT, LACHT AM BESTEN.
(He who laughs last, laughs best.)

Sponge Cakes: No butter or other shortening is used to make sponge cakes. The fresh, good quality ingredients must be at room temperature. For a better cake, sift together dry ingredients three times. Beat the egg whites until stiff but not dry. Some cooks routinely add a pinch of salt to the egg whites before beating them. The cake is baked in an ungreased tube pan in a slow (300-325 degree), preheated oven for about an hour. When the cake is done, invert pan on a wire rack to let the cake cool before removing it from the pan.

- Separate the egg whites and yolks. Put each in its own bowl.
- Beat the egg yolks until lemon colored.
- If the recipe calls for water, blend it with the beaten egg yolks.
- Gradually add sugar to beaten yolks, beating continously.
- Add flavoring and/or grated lemon rind.
- Carefully fold the sifted, dry ingredients into the egg yolk mixture. Mix until well blended.
- Gently fold the beaten egg whites into the egg yolk batter.
- Pour batter into an ungreased tube pan.

Angel Food Cake: Aspiring home makers among the immigrants dreamed of making a perfect angel food cake. With the ingredients and equipment available to them, it was quite a challenge. It seems like a miracle that so many settlers routinely baked beautiful and delectable "high cakes." Use cake flour and fine sugar(not powdered sugar). All ingredients must be fresh. All equipment must be thoroughly cleaned. A pinch of salt may be added to the egg whites before beating them. Bake in a slow (275-325 degree) oven for about an hour or more. When the cake is done, invert the pan on a wire rack, and let the cake cool before removing it.

- Sift the flour 3 to 4 times. Measure after sifting.
- Sift the cream of tartar onto the unbeaten egg whites.
- If salt is used, it is added to the unbeaten egg whites.
- Beat the egg whites until they are stiff, but not dry.
- Add flavoring.
- Add about 2 tablespoons of sugar at a time very slowly to the beaten whites. Continue until they hold a stiff peak.
- Add flour by sifting or sprinkling it a tablespoon or two at a time over the beaten egg whites. Very carefully fold it into the mixture so as little of the air in the egg whites escapes as possible.
- Gently push batter from mixing bowl into an ungreased tube pan, the bottom of which may be lined with clean paper. Take a knife and pull it very gently in a circle or two around the pan through the batter to break up any air bubbles.

> ## *LIEBE MACHT ERFINDERISCH.*
> (Love will find a way.)

BLITZKUCHEN
(LIGHTING CAKE)

Mix ½ pound of butter, 1 cup sugar, 5 eggs, 1½ cups flour, and 2 teaspoons baking powder. Bake in two flat pans. Sprinkle with sugar and cinnamon.

ZIMMTKUCHEN
(CINNAMON CAKE)

Mix 2 eggs, 1 cup sugar, 1 cup butter, 2 cups milk, 4 cups flour, 2 teaspoons baking powder, and 1 teaspoon cinnamon.

DEUTSCHER KAFFEEKUCHEN
(GERMAN COFFEE CAKE)

Take 2¼ cups sifted flour, 3 level tablespoons baking powder, 1 level teaspoon salt, 3 tablespoons melted butter, 2 tablespoons sugar, 1 beaten egg, and milk. Sift the dry ingredients together. Add melted butter and enough milk to the beaten egg to make 1¼ cups. Stir all ingredients together with a spoon to a stiff dough. Pour it into a biscuit pan, spread out and smooth top. Brush the top lightly with melted butter, and sprinkle it with sugar and ground cinnamon. Bake in a hot oven.

EIERLOSER KUCHEN
(EGGLESS CAKE)

Take 1 cup curdled or sour milk, ½ cup lard, 1 cup sugar, 2 cups flour, 1 teaspoon baking powder, 1 teaspoon cinnamon, 1 teaspoon cloves, ½ teaspoon cocoa and mix. Pour into a pan and bake for ½ hour. Bake this cake when the hens are on strike.

EIN-EI-KUCHEN
(ONE EGG CAKE)

Take ¼ cup butter, 1¾ cups flour, ¼ cup sugar, 1 teaspoon baking powder, ½ cup milk, and 1 well beaten egg. Beat butter to a foam, add the egg and sugar, then the flour, baking powder, and milk. Bake for thirty minutes.

FEDERKUCHEN
(FEATHER CAKE)

Mix 1 cup sugar, 3 beaten eggs, ¼ cup butter, 1 cup flour, 2 teaspoons baking powder, 8 tablespoons milk or water, nutmeg, and grated lemon rind. Simple and good.

KOESTLICHER KUCHEN
(DELICIOUS CAKE)

Mix 1 cup sugar, 1/2 cup butter, 2 eggs (beat the egg whites and the egg yolks separately), 1/2 cup milk, 1/2 cup flour, and 1/2 teaspoon baking powder.

GELBER KUCHEN
(YELLOW CAKE)

Mix 3/4 cup sugar, 1/4 cup butter, 4 well beaten egg yolks, 1/4 cup milk, 3/4 cup flour, 1 teaspoon lemon flavoring, and 1 teaspoon soda.

GOLDKUCHEN
(GOLD CAKE)

Use 8 egg yolks, 1 cup sugar, 3/4 cup butter, 1/2 cup milk, 1 1/2 cups flour, and 2 heaping teaspoons baking powder. Flavoring: orange or lemon extract.

AUFLEGEKUCHEN
(LAYER CAKE)

Take 1 tablespoon butter, 1 cup sugar, 1 egg yolk, and 1 egg white beaten until stiff. Set aside. Sift 2 teaspoons of baking powder with 2 1/2 cups flour; mix in 1 cup milk, vanilla, and other ingredients. After baking cover with icing.

—or—

Use 2 cups sugar, 1 cup butter, 2 eggs, and 1 cup milk. Combine 3 cups flour and 2 teaspoons baking powder; sift 3 times. Mix with the other ingredients.

—or—

Cream together ¾ cup butter and ½ cup sugar; then add 4 egg yolks, 3 cups flour, 2 good teaspoons baking powder, 1 cup milk, and some flavoring. Finally, add stiffly beaten egg whites. Pour into 3 layer pans. Bake in a quick hot oven. Any kind of filling is good.

—or—

Mix 1 cup butter, 2 cups sugar, 6 eggs (beat in one at a time), 1 cup milk, 3 cups flour, 2 teaspoons baking powder, and flavor to taste.

DELIKATER KUCHEN
(DELICATE CAKE)

Mix 1 cup butter, 2 cups sugar, 1 cup sweet milk, 3½ cups flour, and 3 teaspoons baking powder. Add 5 stiffly beaten egg whites. Flavor with almond or vanilla.

SILBERKUCHEN
(SILVER CAKE)

Take 1½ cups sugar, ½ cup butter, 3 cups flour, ½ cup milk, 6 egg whites beaten to snow, and 1½ teaspoons of baking powder.

—or—

Use the whites of 8 eggs, 2 cups sugar, ½ cup butter, ¾ cup milk, 1½ cups flour, and 2 heaping teaspoons of baking powder. Flavoring: Almond or lemon extract.

SCHNEEKUCHEN
(SNOW CAKE)

Cream together 2 cups sugar and ½ cup butter. Stir in a cupful of sweet milk. Add 2 cupfuls of flour and 2 teaspoons baking powder. Beat 5 egg whites and stir into dough. Don't bake too quickly.

—or—

Take 3 cups butter, 2 cups sugar, 1 cup milk, 2 cups flour, 1 cup corn starch, and 1½ teaspoons baking powder. Sift together flour, corn starch, and baking powder; cream butter and sugar; alternately add milk and flour mixture. Finally, add 7 egg whites beaten to snow. Add grated lemon rind or vanilla as preferred. Bake slowly for 1 hour.

WEISSER KUCHEN
(WHITE CAKE)

Use 2 cups sugar, 1 cup butter, ½ cup milk, ½ cup water, 3 cups flour, 2 teaspoons baking powder, and the whites of 6 eggs.

—or—

Stir 1 cup butter and 3 cups sugar together until creamy, then add 3 cups flour, 1 teaspoon baking powder, 1 cup corn starch, 1 cup sweet milk, and ¼ teaspoon salt. Beat the whites of 12 eggs until stiff, and fold them into dough. Bake in a moderate oven.

BRAUT-TORTE (VORZUEGLICH)
(BRIDE'S TORTE—EXCELLENT)

Cake: Mix together 1 pound butter, 1 pound grated almonds, 1 pound sugar, 1 pound flour, 12 beaten egg yolks, the grated skin of 1 lemon, and 1 teaspoon allspice. Fold in 12 stiffly beaten egg whites. Bake in 4 greased layer pans in a moderate oven until golden. **Filling:** Melt ¼ pound butter. Stir in ¼ pound sugar, the juice of 4 lemons, and 4 beaten egg yolks.

EIN VOLLER BAUCH, EIN LEERER KOPF.
A FULL BELLY, AN EMPTY HEAD.
(A fat belly, a lean brain.)

Cook over a low heat stirring constantly until mixture thickens. Spread between layers and top of cake.

HOCHZEITSKUCHEN
(WEDDING CAKE)

Beat together 1 cup butter and 3 cups sugar until creamy. Sift the following four times: 3 cups flour, 3 teaspoons baking powder, 1 cup cornstarch, and 1/4 teaspoon salt. Beat the whites of 12 eggs stiff. Mix together with 1 cup sweet milk. Combine ingredients. Bake in a slow oven.

KAKAOKUCHEN
(COCOA CAKE)

Take 1 cup sugar, 1 teaspoon salt, 4 tablespoonfuls butter, 3/4 cup cocoa, 1 egg, 1 cup sour milk, and 1 teaspoon soda. Mix these ingredients with enough flour to make a fairly thin batter. Bake in layers.

SCHOKOLADE-LAGEKUCHEN
(CHOCOLATE LAYER CAKE)

Cake: 1 cup sugar, 1/2 cup butter, 2 eggs, 1/2 cup sweet milk, 2 cups flour, and 1/2 cup baking powder. **Filling:** Put 1/2 cup chocolate in a little cup of milk; let boil, add 1/2 cup sugar, a little piece of butter, salt and flavoring.

TEUFELSFUTTER KUCHEN
(DEVIL'S FOOD CAKE)

Take 1 cup sugar, 1 egg yolk, 1 1/2 cups flour, 1 tablespoon butter, 1 teaspoon baking powder, 2 cakes of bitter chocolate, 1 teaspoon soda, 2 teaspoons vanilla, and 1/2 cup milk.

—or—

Cake: use 2 cups sugar, 3 eggs, 1/2 cup chocolate, 1/2 cup butter, 1 cup hot water, 1 teaspoon soda, 1/2 cup sour milk, 2 teaspoons baking powder, and 3 cups flour. **Filling:** Cook 1/2 cup sweet milk, 1/2 cup butter, and 2 cups sugar to a syrup. Add flavoring according to taste. Beat until creamy. Spread between the layers and on top of cake.

—or—

Cream 2 cups brown sugar and 3/4 cup butter; add 2 whole eggs and 1/2 cup sour milk or cream. Dissolve 1/4 bar of chocolate and 1/2 teaspoon soda in 1/2 cup boiling water. Mix all ingredients together with 3 cups flour.

NELKENKUCHEN
(CLOVES CAKE)

Use 1 cup sugar, 1/2 cup butter, 1 teaspoon cloves, 1 teaspoon cinnamon, 1 teaspoon nutmeg, 1 cup chopped raisins, 1 teaspoon soda, 1 cup sour milk, and 4 cups flour.

MOLASSESKUCHEN
(MOLASSES CAKE)

Combine 1/2 cup sugar, 1/2 cup lard, some salt, 2 egg yolks, 1 cup molasses, 1 cup water, 1 teaspoon soda, 1 teaspoon cinnamon, 1 teaspoon ground cloves, and enough flour to make a batter. Makes 3 layers. Bake in moderate oven. Glaze.

WEICHER MOLASSESKUCHEN
(SOFT MOLASSES CAKE)

Mix 1 cup molasses, 1 cup sour cream, 1 egg, 1 teaspoon soda dissolved in hot water, 1 teaspoon cinnamon or ginger, and 2 scant cups of flour.

GEWUERZKUCHEN
(SPICE CAKE)

Cake: Take 2 eggs, 1 cup brown sugar, ½ cup butter, ½ cup molasses, 1 cup sour milk, 1 teaspoon soda, 1 teaspoon each of cinnamon, cloves, nutmeg, and baking powder, and 2½ cups flour. Mix together, and bake in layers. **Filling:** Cook 2 cups sugar and ½ cup water until the syrup spins a thread when dropped from a spoon. Pour it slowly over 2 beaten egg whites. Add 1 cup chopped raisins.

—or—

Take 1 cup syrup, 1 cup sugar, ⅔ cup butter, 1 cup sour milk, 3 eggs, 1 tablespoons soda, 1 teaspoon nutmeg, 1½ teaspoonsful cinnamon, 1 teaspoonful cloves, and 3 cups flour.

—or—

Take 3 eggs, 1½ cups sugar, 1 cup butter, ½ cup milk, ½ cup raisins, 2 teaspoons baking power, 1 tablespoon cinnamon, some nutmeg, and 2½ to 3 cups flour. Bake in a not too hot oven.

—or

Take ½ cup butter, 1 cup sugar, 2 cups flour, 2 level teaspoons baking powder, ½ teaspoon nutmeg, ½ teaspoon cinnamon,

MAN SOLL DEN TEUFEL NICHT AN DIE
WAND MALEN.

ONE SHALL NOT PAINT THE DEVIL
ON THE WALL.

(Sufficient unto the day is the evil thereof.)

¾ cup water, ½ teaspoon salt, and 4 egg yolks. Cream the butter and sugar well; add the egg yolks. Sift the flour, baking powder, spices, and salt together three times, then add it with water to butter mixture.

—or—

Mix ¾ cup butter, 1½ cups sugar, 3 cups flour, 3 teaspoons baking powder, ¾ cup sweet milk. Add the whites of 4 eggs beaten to snow. Cloves, cinnamon, nutmeg, and grated chocolate may be added.

—or—

Cream 1 cup butter and 1½ cups sugar, add 3 beaten egg yolks, 1 cup sour milk, 1 full teaspoon baking soda, 1 heaping cup raisins, 1 cup nuts, 3 cups flour, and 1 teaspoon each of cloves, nutmeg, and cinnamon. Then, add 3 stiffly beaten egg whites.

—or—

Take 1 cup butter, 1½ cups sugar, 3 eggs, 1 cup sour milk, 1 full teaspoon soda, 1 heaping cup raisins, 1 cup currants, some candied lemon peel, 3 cups flour, and 1 teaspoon allspice.

SCHACHBRETT KUCHEN (CHECKERBOARD CAKE)

Light colored part: 2 eggs, 1 cup white sugar, ¼ cup butter, ½ cup milk, 1½ cups flour, and 1½ teaspoons baking powder
Dark colored part: Just like the light colored part, only use dark brown sugar instead of white sugar. Use two Layer Pans. In the first layer pan pour a light colored ring of batter, then a dark colored ring of batter, until the pan is full. In the second layer pan pour a dark colored ring of batter first, than a light colored ring of batter, until the pan is full. One should watch that the rings are pretty equal. Lay a light colored ring, then a dark colored ring on top of one another.

MARMORKUCHEN
(MARBLE CAKE)

White part: Cream 1½ cups sugar and ½ cup butter; add ½ cup sweet milk, 1 teaspoon soda or baking powder, 2½ cups flour, and 4 egg whites. **Dark part:** Cream 1 cup brown or white sugar, ½ cup dark syrup, and ½ cup butter. Add to this ½ cup sweet milk, 1 teaspoon soda, 2½ cups flour, 4 egg yolks, and 1 tablespoon each of cloves, cinnamon, and nutmeg. Alternate putting dark batter and white batter into the pan. Bake 1 hour.

—or—

White batter: 2 cups sugar, 1 cup butter, ½ cup milk, 3 cups flour, 3 teaspoons baking powder, and the whites of 7 eggs. **Dark batter:** 3 cups dark brown sugar, 1 cup butter, 1 cup sweet milk, 3 cups flour, the yellows of 7 eggs, 2 teaspoons cinnamon and allspice, 1 teaspoon nutmeg, and 1 teaspoon cloves. Bake in layers, alternating white and dark batter.

SCHICHTEN GELEEKUCHEN
(LAYER JELLY CAKE)

Mix 1 cup sugar, ½ cup butter, 3 eggs, ½ cup sweet milk, 2 cups flour, 2 heaping teaspoons baking powder, and lemon extract as preferred.

GELEEKUCHEN
(JELLY CAKE)

Take 3 cups sugar, 1 cup butter, 5 cups flour, 1 cup milk, 5 eggs (The egg yolks and whites are beaten separately), 1 teaspoon soda, and 2 spoons cream of tartar. Bake in thin layers. Spread each baked layer with currant jelly. Lay 3 or 4 layers one on top of the other.

KOKOSNUSS-JELEE-KUCHEN
(COCONUT JELLY CAKE)

Mix 1 cup sweet milk, 1 cup butter, 1 cup corn starch, 2 cups sugar, 2 teaspoonful baking powder, and the whites of 5 eggs. Bake in 3 layers. For the "jelly" take 1 pound of sugar and cook it until it's like candy. Let it cool; then add the foam of 2 eggs and 1½ cup grated coconut. Finally, spread the jelly on the cake.

ROLLKUCHEN
(ROLLED CAKE)

Take 3 well beaten egg yolks, 1 cup flour, 1 cup sugar, 2 teaspoons baking powder, and 2 teaspoons milk. Mix the sugar, milk, and beaten egg yolks together; then add the flour and baking powder. At last, add 5 stiffly beaten egg whites. Bake in 2 baking tins. When cakes are baked, remove them from the oven, and put them on paper. Spread jelly on them. Roll up.

—or—

Use 5 eggs, 1 cup sugar, 2 cups flour, 2 teaspoons baking powder, and lemon extract. Bake in greased pan. Turn out onto a damp cloth, and spread with jelly or lemon filling. Then quickly roll it up.

KOKOSNUSSKUCHEN
(COCONUT CAKE)

Take 1 cup coconut, 4 eggs, 1 cup butter, 1 teaspoon baking powder, 1 cup sugar, 3½ cups flour, 1 cup milk, and lemon extract.

—or—

Cake: 3 cups flour, ½ cup butter, 1 cup sugar, 1 cup milk, 5 eggs, and baking powder. Cream butter and sugar until it's white. Then add one egg after the other. After that, alternately add milk and flour. Pour batter into 4 layer pans. Bake in a good hot oven. **Icing:** Beat 4 egg whites until stiff and mix with 1 pound powdered sugar. Spread icing over the cake and sprinkle coconut over it.

MACRONENKUCHEN
(MACAROON CAKE)

Cake: For 1 pound flour, use 3/4 pound butter, 1/4 pound sugar, and 1/2 wine glass of cold water; mix to a stiff dough. Roll out; put it into a pan. **Topping:** 1 pound ground nuts, 1 pound sugar, juice and grated peel of 1 lemon, some cinnamon, and the stiffly beaten whites of 7 eggs. Heat butter and nuts stirring constantly; remove from heat and blend in the lemon and cinnamon. Finally, fold in the egg whites. Spread mixture on cake dough. Bake in moderate oven.

KORINTHEKUCHEN
(CURRANT CAKE)

Use 1 cup butter, 2 cups sugar, 4 eggs, 3 1/2 cups flour, 1 cup sour milk, 2 cups currants, some soda, and 1 teaspoon lemon extract.

ROSINENKUCHEN
(RAISIN CAKE)

Use 1 1/2 cups sugar, 2/3 cup butter, 2/3 cup milk, 3 cups flour, 4 eggs, 1 pound raisins, and 1 1/2 teaspoons baking powder.

ALTE LIEBE ROSTET NICHT.

OLD LOVE DOESN'T GET RUSTY.

(An old flame never dies.)

NUSSKUCHEN
(NUT CAKE)

Use 1 cup pecans, 1 cup raisins, 1 cup butter, 3/4 cup milk, 2 1/2 cups sugar, 3 1/2 cups flour, 5 eggs, and 2 teaspoons baking powder.

—or—

Use 1 cup sugar, 1/2 cup butter, 3 eggs, the grated peel and juice of one lemon, 1 cup nuts, 1/2 cup milk, 2 cups flour, and 1 teaspoon baking powder. Bake in a pan.

AUFLEGEKUCHEN MIT ORANGER FUELLUNG
(LAYER CAKE WITH ORANGE FILLING)

Cake: 10 egg yolks, 1/2 cup butter, 1/2 cup sweet milk, 2 cups flour, and 2 teaspoons baking powder. **Orange filling:** Combine 1 1/2 cups sugar, 1 cup cream or milk, cook until creamy, beat until stiff. Add orange extract.

—or—

Cake: Cream 1 cup sugar and 1/2 cup butter. Add 4 eggs, 1/2 cup milk, 1 1/2 cups flour, and 1 1/2 teaspoons baking powder. Save the white of 1 egg and a little from another egg. Bake. **Icing:** Make an icing out of the egg whites and powdered sugar. Put icing on the cake while it is still warm. Cut oranges into thin slices and lay on the cake while quite warm.

ANANASKUCHEN
(PINEAPPLE CAKE)

Cake: Take the whites of 6 eggs, 1 cup milk, 1 1/2 cups sugar, 2 1/2 cups flour, 1/2 cup butter, vanilla, and baking powder. Bake in layers. **Filling:** The filling is made of the whites of three eggs, 1 cup powdered sugar, and a can of pineapple.

KARTOFFELKUCHEN
(POTATO CAKE)

Use 1 cup butter, 2 cups sugar, 1 cup crushed pecans, 1/2 cup chocolate, 1 cup cooked, grated potatoes, 4 egg whites, 1 teaspoon cinnamon, some nutmeg and cloves, and 2 cups flour mixed with 2 teaspoons baking powder. Bake one hour or longer if necessary. Make a filling with chocolate for it.

EILE MIT WEILE.

(Haste makes waste.)

KAFFEEKUCHEN
(COFFEE CAKE)

Use 1 1/2 cups sugar, 1 cup lard, 1/2 cup molasses, 1/2 cup milk, 1/2 cup strong coffee, 1 egg, 1 teaspoon soda, 1 teaspoon each of cloves, cinnamon, and nutmeg, 1 pint raisins, and 3 cups flour.

—or—

Mix 1/2 cup butter, 1 cup brown sugar, 1 cup molasses, 1 cup strong black coffee, 1 beaten egg, 4 cups flour, 1 heaping teaspoon baking powder, 1 tablespoon cinnamon, and 1 tablespoon ground cloves. Sprinkle 2 pounds seedless raisins and 1/4 pound finely chopped candied lemon peel with flour; mix into batter. Bake for 1 hour.

—or—

Take 2 cups brown sugar, 4 eggs, 1 cup cold coffee, 1 cup butter, 1 cup molasses, 2 cups raisins, 2 teaspoons cloves, 1/2 teaspoon nutmeg, 1 teaspoon soda, and 4 cups flour.

TASSENKUCHEN
(CUPS CAKE)

Take 1 cup butter, 2 cups sugar, 3 cups flour, 4 eggs, 1 cup milk, 1 teaspoon baking powder, and 1 teaspoon vanilla. Cream the eggs and sugar to a foam, then slowly add the other ingredients. Bake from 1 to 1½ hours.

FEINER KUCHEN
(FINE CAKE)

Take 1 cup butter, 2 cups sugar, 1 cup sweet milk, 3 cups flour, 2 teaspoons baking powder, and preferred flavoring. Bake in tube pan or in 4 layer pans.

GOLDKUCHEN
(GOLD CAKE)

Use 1 cup butter, 2 cups sugar, 8 egg yolks, 3 cups flour, 1 cup milk, 2 teaspoons baking powder, and some lemon juice. Bake 1 hour.

PFUNDKUCHEN
(POUND CAKE)

Use 10 eggs, 1 pound butter, 1 pound sugar, and 1 pound flour.

EINFACHER KUCHEN
(SIMPLE CAKE)

Take 3 cups sugar, 1 cup butter, 1 cup milk, 4 cups flour, and 6 eggs (the whites beaten to a foam). Bake in a tube pan.

SONNENAUFGANG KUCHEN
(SUNRISE CAKE)

Take 3/4 cup butter, 2 teaspoons baking powder, 1/2 cup sugar, 2 teaspoons of lemon extract, 2 1/2 cups flour, 9 egg yolks, and 1 cup milk. Cream butter and sugar; add beaten egg yolks, then add flour, milk, flavoring, and baking powder. Bake the thick batter slowly for fifty to sixty minutes.

KAESEKUCHEN
(CHEESE CAKE)

Pastry: Mix together 2 1/2 cups flour, 1/2 teaspoon salt; blend in 6 tablespoons butter and the grated rind of 1/2 lemon; mix in 4 beaten eggs, 1 cup milk, and 1 tablespoon dried yeast dissolved in the milk. Spread on the bottom and sides of a greased round pan. **Filling:** Blend 3 tablespoons of melted butter and 1 tablespoon flour; gradually add 1/2 cup boiling milk. Stir until thick. Cool. Blend in 2 cups soft cheese (cream cheese or pot cheese), 4 beaten eggs, 1 cup sugar, and the grated rind of one lemon. Beat until smooth. Pour into pastry. Bake in a medium oven for about an hour and ten minutes.

ENGELKUCHEN
(ANGEL CAKE)

Sift together five times 11 tablespoons flour and 1 level teaspoon of cream of tartar. Beat 11 egg whites until stiff, fold in 11 tablespoons of sugar, then cut the flour mixture into the egg whites with a knife. Lay a thin piece of ungreased paper in the bottom of a tube pan, put the batter on it. Bake it about forty minutes. There is a danger of the cake top becoming too dark; therefore, put a pan of water on the rack below the baking cake.

> *HUNGER IST DER BESTE KOCH.*
> HUNGER IS THE BEST COOK.
> (Necessity is the best teacher.)

SCHWAMMKUCHEN
(SPONGE CAKE)

Beat 3 egg yolks until light; gradually add 1 cup sugar. Sift together 1¼ cups flour and 1 teaspoon baking powder; add gradually to the egg yolks; mix until blended. Fold 3 stiffly beaten egg whites and 1 teaspoon grated lemon rind into batter. Bake in ungreased pan in moderate oven for about forty-five minutes.

—or—

Sift together 2 cups flour and 1 teaspoon baking powder. Beat 6 egg yolks and 6 tablespoons of cold water until foamy; add 2 cups sugar and ½ of the flour mixture; beat until smooth; fold in 3 stiffly beaten egg whites; slowly mix in the other ½ of the flour mixture; fold in 3 more stiffly beaten eggs whites and preferred flavoring. Put in ungreased pan, and bake in a moderate to hot oven.

FRUCHTKUCHEN
(FRUIT CAKE)

Beat together 2 cups sugar, ¾ cup butter, and 3 egg yolks for awhile. Then add 1 cup milk and 3 stiffly beaten egg whites, 3 cups sifted flour, and 3 teaspoons baking powder. Lightly flour ½ pound candied lemon peels cut into fine strips, 1 cup seedless raisins, and the same amount of currants; add to the batter and mix. Bake in a not too hot oven.

—or—

Take 1 pound butter, 12 eggs (the whites are beaten separately), 1 pound sugar, 1 pound pecans, 1 pound raisins, 1 pound currants, 1/4 pounds flour, 1 teaspoon baking powder, 1 glass brandy, and 1 teaspoon allspice. Bake in a moderate oven.

—or—

Use 1 pound flour, 1 pound raisins, 2 pounds currants, 4 eggs, 1 teaspoon each of a variety of spices, 1 glass of wine, 1 cup sugar, 1 cup molasses, 1 glass brandy, 1½ cups nuts, 1 teaspoon soda, 1 cup candied peels, ½ cup coconut, and 1 cup coffee.

—or—

Use 2 cups sugar, 1 cup butter, 4 eggs, 1 cup sour milk, 5 cups flour, 1 teaspoon soda, 1 pound raisins, ½ pound candied peels, ½ pound figs, ½ pound dates, 3 cups nuts, 1 teaspoon cloves, 1 teaspoon allspice, 1 teaspoon cinnamon, 1 glass wine, and 1 glass brandy.

—or—

Use 1 pound brown sugar, 3/4 pound butter, 8 eggs, ½ pound candied lemon peel, 1 pound raisins, 1 pound currants, 1 pound dates, 1 pound figs, ½ cup molasses, 1 wine glass of wine or brandy, 1 pound flour, 1 teaspoon each of cloves, nutmeg, and cinnamon, and 1 piece of soda the size of a pea. This makes a big cake that keeps for a year.

WER ZUERST KOMMT, MAHLT ZUERST.

WHO COMES FIRST (TO THE MILL)

GRINDS FIRST.

(The early bird gets the worm.)

—or—

Cream 1 pound butter and 2 cups sugar; beat in 12 beaten eggs; add 2 teaspoons cinnamon, 1 teaspoon each of cinnamon, nutmeg, allspice, and cloves, 1 teaspoon soda, 4 cups flour, 1 cup milk, and 1 cup whiskey. Dredge 1 pound currants, 1 pound raisins, 1 pound figs, 1 pound dates, 1 pound candied peels, 2 cups pecans, 2 cups almonds, 1 cup cherries, and 1 cup pineapple in flour. Mix fruit and 1 cup molasses into the batter.

SCREIBEN SIE IHR LIEBLINGSREZEPT HIER!
WRITE YOUR FAVORITE RECIPE HERE!

_____
_____
_____
_____
_____
_____
_____
_____
_____
_____
_____
_____
_____
_____
_____
_____
_____
_____
_____
_____
_____
_____
_____
_____
_____
_____
_____
_____

PASS IT ON TO THE NEXT GENERATION!

KLEINES BACKWERK

LITTLE PASTRY

"Koch Tips" From Long Ago

When baking cakes or small buns, don't grease the pan, just coat it with flour.

To make gingerbread and molasses cookies tastier, add a little grated orange peel.

Cool cookies thoroughly before storing.

To keep soft cookies moist and crisp cookies dry, store each separately in tightly covered tins or jars.

If crisp cookies become soft, they may be heated again until crisp.

If soft cookies get hard, put a cup of boiling water in the box. The steam will soften them. When the water stops steaming, take it out of the box and replace it with more steaming water. Repeat this process until the cookies are soft.

Boil a pastry brush often to keep it from getting rancid.

Sweeten whipped cream with honey for added flavor. It keeps whipped cream firmer too.

If you are interrupted while making cookies, don't worry! Cover the bowl with a damp cloth and the dough will stay soft.

If raisins are allowed to stand in hot water a few minutes, they will not stick to the food chopper when one grinds them.

A little of any spice goes a long way. Don't be heavy-handed.

To "chop" nuts quickly, place them on a board under a piece of heavy paper or a cloth. Then "chop" the nut meats by rolling them with a kitchen rolling pin.

Flour both the rolling pin and the surface on which cookie dough is to be rolled.

Make round cookies without rolling out the dough by dropping dough from a spoon onto a pan. Then flatten it with a glass.

Cut as many cookies as possible from each batch of rolled out dough. After cookie cutter is dipped in flour, be sure to shake it out well before cutting a cookie.

DAS BACKEN EINFACHER MACHEN (MAKING BAKING SIMPLE)

Each December the big frenzy of cookie baking began. Throughout the month the aroma of cookies in the oven filled the house. A variety of cookies had to be ready for Christmas, since guests had to be offered more than one kind. Cookies such as *Pfeffernuesse* and *Lebkuchen* were baked in early December, because they needed to be stored longer to improve their flavor. Since cinnamon stars, sugar cookies, and others tasted better soon after baking, they weren't made until later in the month. The frenzy ended by December 24 with lots of good cookies to eat, and an assortment of decorated cookies ready for the Christmas tree.

Good quality and fresh ingredients are the secret to cookie making success. Before mixing the dough, assemble all ingredients at room temperature. Choose a baking sheet and grease it with unsalted shortening. Preheat oven to 350-400 degrees. Watch cookies while baking, because they bake quickly, and some burn readily. The bottoms of molasses cookies especially tend to burn.

Butter cookie dough mixing:
- Thoroughly mix shortening, sugar, eggs, and other ingredients the recipe may call for such as syrup, honey, or melted chocolate.
- Stir liquid and flavoring into the mixture.
- Sift together flour, baking powder or soda, and salt. Add these to the mixture. If the recipe calls for spices, add them as well. Mix thoroughly.

MORGEN STUNDE HAT GOLD IM MUNDE.
THE MORNING HOUR HAS GOLD
IN THE MOUTH.
(The early bird catches the worm.)

- Add and mix in other fruits or nuts as the recipe requires.
- The final step in the cookie making process depends on the kind of cookies being made. Refer to information about drop, roll, or molded cookies for the last steps.

Drop Cookies: Whoever thought of drop cookies is to be highly regarded, because cookie baking became so much easier. See the butter cookie instructions above for the first steps.

- Drop cookie dough by teaspoonfuls onto a greased baking sheet.
- Put into the oven to bake for about 10 to 20 minutes.
- Remove cookies from the baking sheet.
- Cool on a wire rack before storing.

Roll Cookies: The early Texan-German settlers favored roll cookies. The dough may be cut into varied shapes, and decorated with nuts, dried fruits, or sprinkled with sugar before baking. Brushing the cookie with cream or evaporated milk before baking, makes it glossy. Freshly cut roll cookies may also be brushed with unbeaten egg whites and sprinkled with sugar and cinnamon before baking. Plain cookies—after baking—may either be frosted or decorated with colored sugar. Check the butter cookie entry for the initial steps.

- Make a smooth ball of the dough.
- To roll more easily some cookie dough must sit overnight or be refrigerated. Other dough can be rolled right after mixing.

- Use as litttle flour as possible when rolling cookie dough.
- To prevent sticking, rub flour onto the rolling pin, and dip cookie cutter in flour. Shake off the excess.
- Roll out a little dough at a time on a lightly floured board.
- The thinner the dough; the crisper the cookie.
- Place cutout cookies on a greased baking sheet and bake for about ten minutes.
- Carefully remove from baking sheet.
- Cool on a wire rack before storing.

Molded Cookies: A molded cookie, a delicious buttery cookie, has long been a German favorite. For the first steps see the entry for Butter cookies.

- Use hands to form the dough into little balls or straight, slim, stick-candy like pieces.
- The balls may be flattened with a glass and criss-crossed with a fork.
- The stick-candy pieces may be formed into crescents, wreaths, circles, and more.
- Place the shaped cookie on a greased baking sheet and bake for ten to twelve minutes.
- Some of these cookies are baked until set, but not brown.
- Remove from baking sheet.
- Cool on a wire rack before storing.

MANDELKRAENZE (ALMOND WREATHS)

Beat 3/4 pound butter to a froth; add 3 egg yolks, 1/2 pound sugar, and 1 pound flour; mix thoroughly. Shape into little wreaths, brush with egg whites and sprinkle with finely chopped almonds, cinnamon, and sugar.

MANDELPLAETZE
(ALMOND DROPS)

Cream 2 ounces of butter; add ½ pound sugar, 4 eggs, 2 ounces of ground almonds, and the grated rind of ½ lemon; gradually blend in ½ pound of sifted flour. Drop from teaspoon onto greased pan. Bake in a moderate oven.

—or—

Mix 2 ounces of melted chocolate, 2 lightly beaten eggs, 1 cup sugar, 1 teaspoon vanilla extract, and 1½ cups blanched chopped almonds. Sift together 3 times: 1 cup flour, 1 teaspoon baking powder, and ½ teaspoon each of salt and cinnamon; mix with egg mixture. Drop by teaspoonful onto a buttered pan. Bake in a moderate oven.

KLEINE ANISKUCHEN
(LITTLE ANIS CAKES)

Use 8 eggs, 2 pounds sugar, 1½ teaspoons baking powder, some anis, cinnamon, and enough flour to make a soft dough.

—or—

Beat together 2 pounds sugar and 9 beaten egg yolks. Gradually add 2½ pounds flour, 1 teaspoon baking powder, and 2 teaspoons ground anis seeds; add 9 stiffly beaten egg whites. Let dough stand overnight. In the morning, roll, cut out, and bake.

BISCUITPLAETZCHEN
(BISCUIT COOKIES)

Mix 4 eggs, ½ pound sugar, lemon juice, and some baking powder. Put by spoonfuls on pan.

BUTTERMILCHKUCHEN
(BUTTERMILK CAKES)

Put 2 teaspoons of soda into 2 cups buttermilk; mix with 1 cup butter and 4 cups creamed sugar; use enough flour to make a dough that can be rolled out.

BUTTERPLAETZCHEN
(BUTTER COOKIES)

Mix ¾ pound butter, 2 eggs, ½ pound sugar, preferred flavoring; add 1 pound flour; shape into little flat round cakes; sprinkle with sugar and cinnamon; bake. Makes about fifty cookies.

BUTTERGEBACKENES KLEINES BACKWERK
(LITTLE BAKED BUTTER PASTRY)

Mix 1 pound butter, 3 to 5 eggs, 2 pounds sugar, 1 cup milk, flavoring, and about 2¼ pounds flour. Roll, then cut out. Makes 4 gallons.

ZIMMTSTERNE
(CINNAMON STARS)

Cream 1 pound sugar and ½ pound butter; beat in 4 eggs one at a time; mix until light; add 2 cups flour sifted with 2 teaspoons baking powder, and ⅛ ounce of ground cinnamon. Roll out the dough. More flour may need to be added to roll out the dough. Sprinkle sugar over dough; cut out stars. One pound grated almonds may be added to the dough.

—or—

Beat 6 egg whites until stiff; gradually blend in 1 pound powdered sugar and the grated rind of 1 lemon; beat for 15 minutes. Put a part of this mixture aside on a saucer to use for a glaze. Mix the remainder with 1 pound ground nuts and 1 tablespoon cinnamon. Shape stars one at a time out of the mixture with some powdered sugar sprinkled on the baking surface. Bake at a low heat. When done, glaze with the reserved egg white mixture. Return to the oven until the glaze is dry.

SCHOKOLADENKUCHEN (CHOCOLATE CAKES)

Take ½ cup butter, ½ cup sugar, 1 cup pecans, 1 cup cocoa, 3 eggs, 1 teaspoon baking powder, and enough flour to make a dough to roll out.

NELKENKUCHEN (CLOVE CAKES)

Take 2 cups flour, ½ cup molasses, ½ cup butter, ½ cup milk, 2 eggs, 2 cups raisins, 1 teaspoon soda, ½ teaspoon each of cloves, cinnamon, allspice, and nutmeg.

KOKOSNUSSTROPFEN (COCONUT DROPS)

Take ½ cup butter, ½ cup coconut, 1 cup sugar, 1 tablespoon milk, 1 egg, a level teaspoon baking powder, and about 1¼ cups flour. Drop dough from teaspoon onto greased pan.

MIT EINEN VOLLEN BACKEN SPRECHEN.
(Speak with one's mouth full.)

KOKOSNUSSKUCHEN
(COCONUT CAKES)

Take 2 cups sugar, 1 cup butter, 2 cups grated coconut, 3 beaten eggs, 1 teaspoon baking powder, and enough flour to make a dough just stiff enough to roll out. Bake in a moderate oven.

KORINTHENKUCHEN
(CURRANT CAKES)

Take 1½ cups sugar, 1 cup butter, ½ cup sour milk, 1 cup currants, 1 teaspoon each of cinnamon, cloves, and nutmeg. Dissolve 1 teaspoon soda in the sour milk. Use enough flour to make a dough to roll out.

KLEINE GEFUELLTE DATTELKUCHEN
(LITTLE FILLED DATE CAKES)

Dough: Take 1 cup sugar, 1 cup lard and butter, ½ cup sweet milk, 2 cups oatmeal, ½ teaspoon soda, 2 cups flour, and 1 teaspoon baking powder. Roll out the dough into a thin sheet, then cut out little cookies. Put filling on one cookie and put another cookie on top of the filling. Press together and bake.
Filling: Cook 1 cup dates and one cup water to a soft puree. Some lemon extract may be added if desired.

EIERPLAETZCHEN
(EGG COOKIES)

Mix ½ cup butter, 1 pound sugar, 7 finely grated hard boiled egg yolks, 2 whole raw eggs, 1 teaspoon baking powder, and 1 pound flour. Roll and cut out cookies. Bake until half brown.

EIERLOSEPLAETZCHEN
(EGGLESS COOKIES)

Take 2½ cups of sugar, 1 cup each of lard and milk, 1 teaspoon soda, a pinch of salt, and 2 teaspoons vanilla. Use enough flour to make a dough one can easily roll out.

—or—

Take 1 cup sour cream, 1¼ cups sugar, 1 knife point of salt, 1 level teaspoon of soda, 2¼ cups flour, and lemon extract according to taste. Roll out dough and cut out cakes. Bake in a medium hot oven.

KLEINE FRUCHTKUCHEN (LITTLE FRUIT CAKES)

Mix 2 cups sugar, 2 big eggs, ½ cup butter, 1 cup raisins, 1 teaspoon cloves, 1 teaspoon baking powder, and ½ teaspoon soda mixed with 2 cups flour. Roll out dough; cut into cakes with a glass. Bake in moderate oven.

—or—

Use 1 cup butter, 1½ cups brown sugar, 1 cup pecans, ½ cup raisins, 2 eggs, 1 big tablespoon of sour milk, 1 teaspoon soda, and enough flour to make a dough to roll out.

—or—

Take 2 cups sugar, 1 cup butter, 2 cups chopped raisins, 1 cup chopped pecans, 2 eggs, ½ cup sour milk, 1 teaspoon soda, ½ teaspoon nutmeg, ½ teaspoon cinnamon, and enough flour to roll out.

—or—

Take 4 scant cups sugar, 4 eggs, 1 cup butter, ½ cup milk, ½ cup raisins, 1 box coconut, 1 cup pecans, 1 teaspoon baking powder, and enough flour to roll dough out into a thin dough.

INGWERKEKS (GINGER SNAPS)

Heat together 1 cup molasses and 1 cup lard. Mix together 2 eggs and 1 cup sugar. Take 1 tablespoon soda and 1 tablespoon ginger. Mix completely all ingredients with enough flour to make a dough to roll out.

INGWERPLAETZCHEN
(GINGER COOKIES)

Cream 1 cup sugar and 1 cup butter; beat in 1 beaten egg and 1 cup molasses; add 1 teaspoon soda dissolved in ⅓ cup vinegar; mix in 1 teaspoon salt, 1 tablespoon ginger, and enough flour to make a dough stiff enough to roll out. Cut out cookies and bake in a hot oven.

HONIGKUCHEN
(HONEY CAKES)

Bring 2 pounds honey and ½ pound butter to a boil. Take from fire and add 1 teaspoon cloves, 6 ounces of coarsely ground nuts, the grated peel of 1 lemon, and 2 pounds flour. When dough is slightly cooled, mix in 2 teaspoons soda dissolved in a little water. Let the dough set overnight. Roll out about a finger thick. Bake in oven until golden brown.

—or—

Heat 2 quarts honey; mix in 3 pounds sugar; Stir in 2 tablespoons cinnamon, ½ teaspoon cloves, 3 tablespoons baking powder, about 6 pounds of flour, ½ pound nuts, the grated rind of one lemon, and 1 pound candied citron. Roll and cut out cakes. Let stand overnight. Bake.

ALLZUVIEL IST UNGESUND.
TOO MUCH IS UNHEALTHY.
(Enough is as good as a feast.)

HONIGTROPFEN
(HONEY DROPS)

Take 1 cup honey, 1/2 cup sugar, 1/3 cup butter, 1 cup sour milk, 1 egg, 1/2 teaspoon soda, and 4 cups flour. Drop dough from teaspoon onto pan. Bake.

KRINGEL
(RING SHAPED COOKIE)

Cream 1/2 pound sugar and 1/2 pound butter, beat in 1 table-spoon whiskey and 3 beaten egg yolks. Sift together and stir in 1 pound flour and 1 teaspoon baking powder. Shape dough into little circles. Brush with slightly beaten egg whites and sprinkle with chopped nuts, cinnamon, and sugar. Bake.

ZITRONEKRAENZE
(LEMON WREATHS)

Cream 3/4 pound butter and 1 pound sugar; beat in 9 beaten egg yolks and the juice and grated peel of 1 lemon; mix in 2 tea-spoons baking powder and enough flour to make a dough stiff enough to roll out. Cut out. Bake.

MOLASSESKUCHEN
(MOLASSES CAKES)

Bring 1 cup molasses and 1 cup butter or lard to a boil; let cool. Add 1 tablespoon soda, 1 cup chopped pecans, 1 cup sugar, 2 beaten eggs and enough flour to make a dough which rolls easily. Cut out cookies and bake.

—or—

Take 2 eggs, 1 cup sugar, 1 cup molasses, 1 tablespoon butter, 1 teaspoon soda, 1 teaspoon baking powder, 1 teaspoon choco-late, some red pepper, salt, ginger, cinnamon, allspice, and as many nuts as one wishes to use. Add enough flour to make a dough that can be rolled out easily.

—or—

Take 1 cup sugar, 2 cups molasses, 1 cup fat, 1 cup water, 1 teaspoon soda, preferred flavoring, and as much flour as needed to make a dough that rolls out easily.

—or—

Take 1 quart molasses, 2 cups sugar, 1 cup lard, 1 cup sour milk, 1 teaspoon each of cloves, nutmeg, and cinnamon, 2 teaspoons soda and enough flour to make a dough stiff enough for cut out cookies.

NUSSKUCHEN
(NUT CAKES)

Beat together 6 eggs and 4 cups sugar. Add 1 quart chopped nuts and enough flour to make dough that's easy to roll. Mix. Let dough stand six to eight hours before rolling and cutting out cookies. Bake.

HAFERMEHLKEKS
(OATMEAL COOKIES)

Cream ½ cup butter, ½ cup lard, and 1 cup sugar; beat in 2 well beaten eggs and a pinch of salt; mix in ¾ teaspoon cinnamon, ½ teaspoon soda dissolved in 4 tablespoons sweet milk, 2 cups oatmeal, 1 cup raisins or currants, and 2 cups flour. Drop from teaspoon onto greased pan.

HAFERMEHLTROPFEN
(OATMEAL DROPS)

Take 2 cups sugar, 2 cups oatmeal, 2 cups flour, 1 cup butter,

4 eggs, and 1½ teaspoons baking powder. Mix. Drop by spoonfuls on pan and bake in moderate oven.

PFEFFERNUESSE
(SPICE COOKIES)

Beat 1 pound brown sugar and 4 eggs together; combine with 1 teaspoon soda dissolved in 2 tablespoons sour milk; mix in 1 tablespoon cinnamon, ½ tablespoon cloves, ½ quart nuts, ½ cup candied peels, and enough flour to make a dough which rolls easily. Let dough stand overnight; bake the next morning.

WEISSE PFEFFERNUESSE
(WHITE SPICE COOKIES)

Take 1 pound flour, 1 pound sugar, 1 grated nutmeg, 1 tablespoon cinnamon, 4 large eggs, the grated rind of a lemon, some candied citron, 1 scant teaspoon cloves, and 1 scant teaspoon baking powder.

ZUCKERPLAETZCHEN
(SUGAR COOKIES)

Take 1½ cups sugar, 1 cup butter, 2 eggs, 3 tablespoons milk or cream, 1 teaspoon baking powder, and enough flour to make a dough that will roll out. Sprinkle cookies with cinnamon.

—or—

Take 2 cups sugar, 1 cup lard, 3 eggs, 1 cup thick sour milk, 1 teaspoon each of soda and cream of tartar, and 1 tablespoon each of lemon and vanilla extract. Add as much flour as needed to make a dough that will roll out.

—or—

Take 2 cups sugar, 1 cup butter or lard, 6 eggs, 2 teaspoons baking powder, and enough flour to make a stiff dough. Roll out dough; cut cookies in all kinds of shapes. Sprinkle with sugar when taken out of the oven.

WEISSE BAUMKUCHEN (WHITE TREE COOKIES)

Take 2 heaping cups of sugar, 1 cup fat, 1 cup sweet milk, 1/2 cup sour cream, 2 eggs, soda, and enough flour to make a dough which rolls out easily.

TEEKUCHEN (TEA CAKES)

Take 2 eggs, 2 cups sugar, 1 cup fat, 8 tablespoons water, 2 teaspoons baking powder, and a little soda. Use enough flour to make a stiff dough that rolls out easily.

—or—

Take 1 cup butter, 1½ cups sugar, 3 eggs, 1 tablespoon whole milk, 2 teaspoons baking powder, and enough flour to make a dough that rolls out easily.

—or—

Take 4 eggs, 3 cups sugar, 1 cup butter, 2 teaspoons baking powder, nutmeg or cinnamon to suit your taste, ½ cup sweet milk, and enough flour to make a dough that rolls out easily.

SCREIBEN SIE IHR
LIEBLINGSREZEPT HIER!
WRITE YOUR FAVORITE RECIPE HERE!

_____

_____
_____
_____
_____
_____
_____
_____
_____
_____
_____
_____
_____
_____
_____
_____
_____
_____
_____
_____
_____
_____
_____
_____
_____
_____
_____
_____
_____

PASS IT ON TO THE NEXT GENERATION!

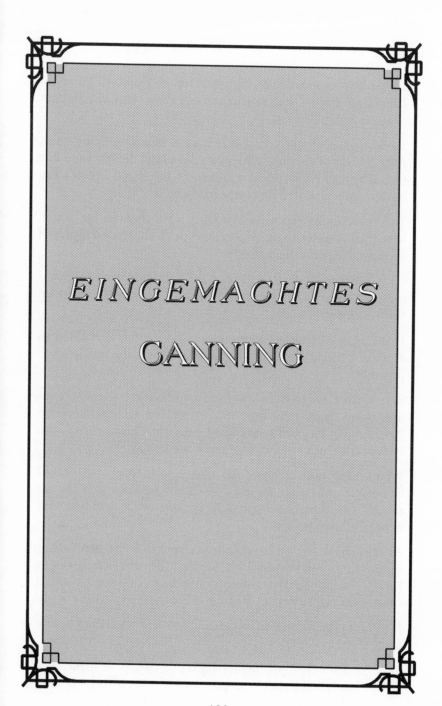

EINGEMACHTES
CANNING

"Koch Tips" From Long Ago

To use less sugar when making jam, let the fruit boil for about 10 minutes longer than usual, then add about ½ of the amount of sugar generally used.

To determine when cooking jelly has reached the jellying stage, pour a little of the hot jelly on a cold plate; draw a wide line through it with the tip of a spoon. If the liquid doesn't run back together, the jellying stage has been reached.

To keep canning jars from cracking, wash them in hot water, heat them and set them on a damp hot cloth. Pour jelly, fruits or vegetables into them slowly.

Only the freshest fruits and vegetables should be used for canning. Canning doesn't improve them; it only preserves them for future use.

If the sizes of fruits or vegetables are different, sort them so that the contents of each jar will be as nearly the same size as possible.

Syrups for canning fruits: Boil sugar and water together 5 minutes using these guidelines: *thin syrup,* use 4 cups water and 2 cups sugar; *medium syrup,* use 4 cups water and 3 cups sugar; *heavy syrup,* use 4 cups water and 4 cups sugar.

When using pint or quart jars that held mayonnaise, peanut butter, or other commercial products, be sure that the jar mouth is so threaded that it will take one of the standard tops which will seal airtight.

Always check jars on hand to make sure that any new lids or rubber rings purchased will fit. See that the rubber ring is right for the particular type of top, and that the screw band is exactly the right depth to fit jar and lid.

It's good practice to boil all canned, nonacid vegetables before using them.

Very hard water may toughen vegetable tissues or make fruit syrup cloudy. Such water can be softened somewhat by boiling and straining it through several layers of muslin. Or, boil water and let it stand until it settles, then pour off the clear water for use.

To remove the "canned taste" from canned vegetables, strain the liquid from the vegetables and pour boiling water over them. Cool vegetables before using.

PUTTING UP fruits and vegetables took time, and it was just plain hard work. Nevertheless, canning and preserving were a necessity, for nothing could be wasted. Vegetables and fruits had to be harvested when in season and canned or preserved to use during the off season. The fact that the time and effort put forth during the harvest season meant that the family would eat better in the winter months ahead was motivation and reward enough for the homemaker. They took pride in the sparkling glass jars filled with colorful vegetables, fruits, jellies, and jams; they liked to show them off.

GRUENE BOHNEN EINZUMACHEN
(CANNING GREEN BEANS)

Cut ends from the beans, and cut beans into salad size pieces. Put them in enough salted water to cover; cook until just tender. Put 1 tablespoon of vinegar in each quart; fill the jar with hot beans. Screw the lid on the jar. The beans keep well. Use to make bean salad.

ROTE RUEBEN EINZUMACHEN
(CANNING RED BEETS)

Cook red beets until done; peel them; cut them into serving pieces. Combine 1 quart water, 1 cup vinegar and ½ cup sugar; bring to a boil. Then pour the beets into the boiling liquid; bring to a boil. Put in jars; seal; store in a dark place.

> *ALIF REGEN FOLGT SONNENSCHEIN.*
> AFTER RAIN FOLLOWS SUNSHINE.
> (Every cloud has a silver lining.)

CHOW-CHOW
(CHOW-CHOW)

Chop 2 quarts of cucumbers and 1 quart green tomatoes. They must stand in salt water overnight. Drain, add 1 quart chopped onion, 1 quart chopped cabbage, 2 quarts vinegar, ½ cup sugar, 1 cup flour, 4 tablespoons dried mustard, and ½ tablespoon red pepper. Bring to a boil. Fill jars with hot mixture. Seal.

SUESSES CORN EINZUMACHEN
(CANNING SWEET CORN)

Take 4 quarts corn kernels and add 1½ quarts water; cook for ten minutes. Then add ½ cup salt and cook three minutes longer. Pour the hot corn into jars and seal.

—or—

Combine 10 heaping cups of corn kernels, 1 cup sugar and 1 cup salt; let stand for ½ hour, then cook for ten minutes. Add no water. Fill jars with hot corn. Seal. When ready to serve, wash, then combine with sugar, milk, 1 tablespoon butter, and 1 tablespoon flour. Bring to a boil.

GOMBO
(GUMBO)

Cut not too hard okra into little pieces; cook them in water; drain. Combine 1 quart okra, ½ cup chopped onions, 1 cup tomatoes cut into pieces, 1 tablespoon vinegar, and 5 to 6 red pepper corns. Cook until the vegetables are tender. Pour into jars. Seal.

DILL GURKEN
(DILL PICKLES)

Wash little cucumbers. Lay a layer of cucumbers in a crock; lay washed green grape leaves and green dill over them. Continue to alternate layers of cucumbers with grape leaves and green dill until the crock is full. Make a brine solution using 1 part salt to 4 parts water. The solution should be so strong that when an egg is put in it, the egg floats. Pour this salty water over the cucumbers in the crock. Let them soak for three days. After three days, remove cucumbers from the brine, wash them, and put them into jars. Sprinkle some red and black pepper corns in each jar. Fill jars with vinegar. Seal tightly.

EINGEMACHTE GURKEN
(CANNED PICKLES)

Let small whole cucumbers lay in strong salt water overnight. In the morning, put them in fresh water with some vinegar, salt, and whole pepper corns. Let them boil somewhat and then pack them with the hot liquid in airtight jars.

SALAT PICKLES
(SALAD PICKLES)

Select pickles from which pieces the size of a 5 cent piece can be cut. Cover 1 gallon of 5 cent piece sized slices with salt water; let stand overnight. Cut 1 pint little white onions into slices. Drain the cucumbers. Rinse the cucumbers and onions; combine with 1/4 pound mustard seeds and 1/2 pound celery seeds; pour hot vinegar over it. When cooled, add 2 tablespoons of fresh olive oil. Store in tightly covered containers. These pickles keep well.

> ## WASSER PREDIGEN UND WEIN TRINKEN.
> ## PREACHING WATER AND DRINKING WINE.
> ### (Not practicing what one preaches.)

SUESS-SAUER EINGEMACHTE GURKEN
(SWEET AND SOUR CANNED PICKLES)

Pour boiling salt water over young green cucumbers; let them stand overnight. In the morning drain; rub the cucumbers with salt and let them stand for two hours. Then combine about ³/₄ quart vinegar and ¹/₄ quart water; add sugar according to taste (about 1 cup), 10 pods of dried red pepper, allspice or dill; bring to a boil; add the cucumbers and bring to a boil again. While hot, put them in canning jars.

EINGEMACHTE GURKEN
(CANNED PICKLES)

Take cucumbers the size of a man's thumb or somewhat thicker, and put them in cold water; let them stand for at least 6 hours. Drain and dry the cucumbers. Pack them into quart jars. To each quart add 1 tablespoon white sugar, 1 tablespoon salt, 1 tablespoon ground mustard, and enough cold uncooked vinegar to cover the cucumbers in the jar. Put a rubber ring on the jar; turn the lid until jar is tightly sealed. They must stand 4 to 6 weeks, until they are quite tasty. These pickles are always good and especially good in salads, because they remain firm and taste like fresh cucumbers.

REIFE EINGEMACHTE SENFGURKEN
(CANNED MUSTARD PICKLES)

Peel large ripe cucumbers; remove seeds; cut into pieces; salt them. Add 1 cup vinegar, 1 cup water, cinnamon as desired,

2 tablespoon dried mustard, 1 tablespoon mustard seeds and 1 tablespoon butter. Cook together until done. Add enough vinegar to cover the cucumbers. Pour into jars and seal.

SAUERKRAUT
(PICKLED CABBAGE)

Choose firm and fresh white cabbage. Remove the outer leaves and shred finely. Then pack alternate layers of cabbage and salt into a crock pressing down firmly so that the juice covers the cabbage. (Salt will draw juice from the cabbage.) Cover the top layer with cabbage leaves, a board, and then a weight (e.g., a stone), heavy enough to make the brine come up to the board. Cover the crock with a piece of cloth secured with a string and store in a cool place. Time for fermentation is from four to six weeks.

EINGEMACHTE TOMATEN
(CANNED TOMATOES)

Scald ripe firm ripe tomatoes in hot water; peel. Cut the tomatoes in quarters. Bring to a boil. Pack in jars while hot. Seal.

GRUENE TOMATEN EINZUMACHEN
(CANNING GREEN TOMATOES)

Wash, scrape, and cut 1 peck of green tomatoes into slices. Sprinkle with salt and let stand overnight. The next morning drain; wash tomatoes in clear water. Put tomatoes in an enamel pot. Combine 1 quart of the best vinegar, 3 pounds brown sugar, 1 tablespoon cinnamon, and 1 tablespoon cloves; pour it over the tomatoes; simmer for two hours. Pour hot tomatoes into jars and seal.

EINGEMACHTE BROMBEEREN
(CANNED BLACKBERRIES)

Combine 3 pounds of picked over big blackberries, 1 pound

> ## *FRISCH GEWAGT IST HALB GEWONNEN.*
> ## (A good beginning is half the battle.)

sugar, ¼ ounce of good stick cinnamon broken into pieces, and some cloves. Cook, stirring gently being very careful not to crush the berries. When they are done, drain syrup from them. Return syrup to the fire and cook it until somewhat thick. Carefully stir the cooked berries back into the hot syrup. Pour into jars and seal.

FEIGEN
(FIGS)

Pick figs with stems before they are completely ripe. Wash, and then cook them in clear water until the figs can be pierced with a straw. Add ¾ pound sugar and cook until thick. Season with cinnamon or lemon. Pour into jars and seal.

—or—

Peel figs and sprinkle sugar over them using ½ pound sugar for each pound of figs. Let them stand overnight. The next morning drain the juice from the figs, and bring it to a boil. Add the figs, and cook until they turn a yellow color. Remove the figs from the syrup; let them dry over night on a platter. Cook the syrup some more. The next morning, put the figs back into the syrup and cook until stiff. Put in jars and seal.

PFIRSICHE IN ZUCKER EINZUMACHEN
(CANNING PEACHES IN SUGAR)

Immerse peaches in boiling water. Remove, and when cool enough to handle, pull off skins. Cut in half and remove the pits. For 3 pounds of peaches, use 3 cups water and ¾ pound sugar. Bring sugar and water to a boil, then lay as many peaches

> # GLUECK UND GLAS, WIE LEICHT BRICH'S
> # LUCK AND GLASS. HOW EASILY THEY BREAK.
> ## (Happiness is as fragile as glass.)

as have room on the surface of the boiling sugar water; when done, put them in hot jars and seal. Continue this process until all peaches are cooked.

KLEINE WILDE PFIRSICHE
(LITTLE WILD PEACHES)

Scrub peaches in cold water. Do not peel or remove pits. Make a syrup with water and sugar. Cook the whole peaches in the syrup until tender. Pack hot in jars, pour syrup over them. Seal.

BRANDY-PFIRSICHE
(BRANDY-PEACHES)

Peel 4 pounds of fruit. Make a syrup of 1½ cups water and 4 pounds sugar. Cook fruit and syrup together for 10 minutes, but cook only a few peaches at a time, so that the fruit isn't mashed. Take the kettle from the fire, add ½ pint brandy. Pack fruit and juice into a jar and seal air tight.

GEPICKELTE PFIRSICHE
(PICKLED PEACHES)

Pour boiling water over 7 pounds of peaches. Let stand in the water until the skins pull off easily. Make a syrup of 1 quart vinegar and 3 pounds sugar. Cook peeled peaches in the syrup until they can be pierced with a fork. Pack peaches into jars. Pour hot syrup over them and seal jars.

> # VIELE KOECHE VERDERBEN DEN BREI.
> (Too many cooks spoil the broth.)

EINGEMACHTE BIRNEN
(CANNED PEARS)

Peel the pears; core; then cut in quarters. Make a syrup of sugar and water. Cook pears until done. Pack them in jars. Pour hot syrup over them and seal jars.

—or—

Peel and core 5 pounds of pears. Slice some lemons. Combine 1½ pounds sugar, ½ quart wine, and ½ quart vinegar; boil and skim. Add pears and lemon slices; cook until tender. Put them in hot jars. After two days, pour the juice from the pears and let it cook throughly. When the syrup is cold, pour it over the pears. Just as in all canning, seal the jars well.

GEPICKELTE MELONENSCHALE
(PICKLED WATERMELON RIND)

Cut the red and green off watermelon rinds. Cut the white rind into strips or cubes. Take 20 cups of prepared watermelon rinds; cover them with water and boil until tender. Combine 2 cups cider vinegar, 7 cups sugar, ¼ teaspoon oil of cloves, and ½ teaspoon cinnamon. Bring to a boil. Drain the rind. Pour syrup over the rind. Let stand overnight. Next morning, pour off the syrup, reheat it, and pour it over the rinds again. Let stand overnight. Do the same thing the following morning. On the third day, heat both the rind and syrup and pour into jars. Seal!

BROMBERRENGELEE
(BLACKBERRY JELLY)

Wash and mash berries. Heat. Press through a jelly cloth to

SICH DAS BROT AM MUNDE ABSPAREN.

TO TAKE THE BREAD
FROM ONE'S OWN MOUTH.

(To pinch and scrape.)

---

remove all the seeds. Use 1 cup of sugar for each pint of juice. Cook rapidly, stirring often until it hangs in sheets from a spoon. Pour into hot jars and seal.

PFIRSCHE MARMELADE
(PEACH JAM)

Take 2 pounds of fresh sliced peaches. Add 2 tablespoons lemon juice and 1 cup water. Cook until tender. Add sugar and cook until thick. Seal in hot clean jars.

TRAUBENGELEE
(GRAPE JELLY)

Heat 1 cup of grape juice made from under ripe grapes to boiling, then slowly add 3/4 to 1 cup sugar. Boil rapidly until the jellying stage is reached. Pour into jars and seal.

PFLAUMEN MARMELADE
(PLUM JAM)

Wash 1 quart plums, add water and cook until skins are tender. Remove the stones. Add 2/3 cup sugar to each cup of plums. Cook quickly until thick. Pour into clean hot jars and seal.

TOMATEN AUFZUBEWAHREN
(TO PRESERVE TOMATOES)

Peel and cut up tomatoes in little pieces. For every 3 cups of cut up tomatoes use 2 cups of sugar. Cook the tomatoes and sugar together fast. Stir often. When the tomatoes begin to stick to the bottom of the pot stir in some lemon juice and keep on cooking for a few more minutes. Pour into jars and seal tight.

EIN SPERLING IN DER HAND
IST BESSER ALS EINE
TAUBE AUF DEM DACH.

A SPARROW IN HAND
IS BETTER THAN A
DOVE ON THE ROOF.

(A bird in the hand is worth
two in the bush.)

SCREIBEN SIE IHR
LIEBLINGSREZEPT HIER!
WRITE YOUR FAVORITE RECIPE HERE!

PASS IT ON TO THE NEXT GENERATION!

INDEX OF RECIPES

123

FLEISCH (MEAT)

GEMUESE (VEGETABLES)

ENDE GUT, ALLES GUT.
ALL'S WELL, THAT ENDS WELL.